Favorable Occasions

FAVORS FOR PARTIES, WEDDINGS, AND HOLIDAYS

By

Beverly Clark

WILSHIRE PUBLICATIONS

Cover Photography: Henry Hamamoto
Book Design: Robin La Fevers
Cover Design and
Black & White Illustrations: Torf Fulton Associates
Typography and Layout: Christine Nolt, Cirrus Design
Editor: Gail Kearns

ISBN: 0-934081-20-4

To everyone who enjoys making their celebrations truly extraordinary.

CONTENTS

ACKNOWLEDGMENTS

As with any book of this magnitude, the end result is the product of many people's hard work. The designs in this book, and perhaps the book itself, would not have been possible without the help of my talented and creative staff members, Robin La Fevers and Rachel Pasley. I would also like to thank all the members of my book team, for whom I am extremely grateful. Victoria Torf-Fulton for her wonderful cover design and black and white illustrations along with her unwavering support and enthusiasm. Christine Nolt for her skill in internal design and layout and her grace under pressure. Gail Kearns for her unerring eye and uncanny ability to catch mistakes, Henry Hamamoto for his consistently beautiful photography, and Hilary Green for her styling talents.

I would also like to add a special thanks to Gail Frigo for believing in the project from the beginning.

FAVORABLE
OCCASIONS

OUR LIVES ARE DECORATED with celebrations, some simple and some extravagant, but each one of them extraordinary in their own unique way. Quiet Thanksgiving dinners, lavish holiday feasts, entertaining for business purposes, or solely for the joy of socializing with our friends, are all equally important aspects of our social selves. We love to infuse each celebration with our own unique brand of style and personally see to every detail to make sure everything is just perfect. This is when special, well-placed favors can become an essential part of entertaining and make the occasion even more memorable.

Beautifully thought-out favors add to the welcoming feel of our table, making our guests feel special and treasured. They are little gifts that tell guests, "Thank you for being a part of our celebration." These tokens of appreciation are appropriate not only for wedding receptions, bridal showers, baby showers, and birthdays, but also for occasions like sit-down dinners with close friends and 4th of July barbecues. Well-placed favors can enliven even the most mundane of occasions, like a boardroom luncheon, faculty gathering, or sales meeting, giving them a more festive

air. Whether a seasoned hostess or just beginning to entertain, opportunities abound to brighten the social and business gatherings of guests and colleagues.

Different celebrations will call for different types of favors. They can be simple or ornate, easy or time consuming. A lot depends on the occasion, your budget, and your energy level. Occasionally, time will be the determining factor, dictating that you go out and purchase favors that can be used 'as is'. At other times, cost will be a primary factor, and you will want to make something that is inexpensive, yet still special. Sometimes the sheer size of the event will determine what direction you take in choosing your favors. If you need three hundred favors, getting them made in a timely fashion can present a challenge, so buying them may be a more convenient option. Even then, you will want them to fit into your budget.

Favors can add color and texture to your table in a variety of unexpected ways. Once you give your creativity free reign, it's amazing to see just how many ways you can take a single, inexpensive element (a glass votive holder or simple placecard, for example) and find hundreds of different, wonderful ways to decorate it. And the decorating can be simple or complex, depending upon your skill level, with stunning results either way.

Topiaries are another remarkably versatile possibility. They can be covered in a variety of materials and mediums, and you can create them to complement almost any décor or theme imaginable. The smaller ones are inexpensive enough to be used as favors for a small to medium size wedding, especially if the bride and her wedding party and friends enjoy getting together and working with their hands. The larger topiaries are better suited to centerpieces, but can also be used for absolutely breathtaking favors, especially for a smaller gathering such as a bridesmaid's luncheon or tea. They work well for dinner party center-pieces or can be used on the wedding reception tables. It is surprisingly easy to pull off a stunningly beautiful creation like this, even with little or no experience.

For a quick, easy and colorful favor, never underestimate the appeal of candy. Especially when put into cute little glass votive cups that can be used for votive candles afterwards. The sheer colorfulness of the candy

fillings adds to the décor. Shimmering little organza bags can hold a multitude of confectionery treats, as can specialized little boxes in a wide assortment of shapes and decorative themes.

The ideas in this book cover a broad range of tastes, from elegant and traditional to sleekly modern and minimalist, and everything in between. Be sure to select projects that are meaningful to you, that you will enjoy making, and that are well-suited to your guests.

Quite often it is all we can do to put an event together, let alone hand make personal favors for each of our guests. Never feel embarrassed about purchasing favors that are already assembled. The following pages contain many great ideas for favors that require little or no effort and still make very nice thank you gifts for your guests.

MAKING YOUR FAVORS

*T*HE GOOD NEWS is that a number of the favor ideas in this book can be made very quickly and inexpensively. Many of them can be put together for less than three dollars each and, when using a production line process, in only a few minutes per favor. In fact, we have special indexes in the back, which list these favor ideas for you. In "Thirty Minute Specials" we list favors that require no more than thirty minutes per dozen. We also have our favorite, "Favors on a Budget," that shows just how many beautiful things are available at a very reasonable cost. Many of the glass votive candle holders featured in this book can be purchased on sale for around fifty cents each. You should never let the lack of time or a small budget be a reason for eliminating favors from your celebration.

In order to help you make the most informed decision when selecting which favor to use, we have set up a rating system for the ideas described in this book. On each instruction page there will be a list of "ingredients", as well as the basic instructions. Each favor is also rated as to its difficulty — whether it is something suited to a beginner or recommended for more advanced skills. An approximate cost range is also indicated, allowing you

to effectively budget and decide whether or not this individual favor is suited to the occasion you have in mind. Estimated time involved is also shown.

If you are already involved in crafts, you will no doubt have many of the supplies you will need on hand. If not, now is a good time to begin building up a reserve of crafting materials that you will use time and time again — from the perfect pair of scissors to a wide collection of ribbons, papers, and a variety of glues. Buy the best quality you can afford so that your tools will withstand the test of time and usage.

If your budget allows, indulge yourself in the joys of using luxurious, high quality materials: vibrant colors, rich textures, unusual trims. Since many of these projects require only small bits of fabric, look into fine quality remnants as a possible way to save money while enjoying high quality. It can also be a nice way to use up fabric scraps you already have at your disposal.

When you begin, make sure you have everything you need for your favors project close at hand. Use the materials list as a "checklist" if you like. Read through the instructions first in order to be certain you understand the steps. If you are going to be making more than one favor at a time (and you probably will), set up the process like an assembly line and do them in lots of ten or twelve. The whole procedure will go much more quickly. (Note: The time listed in each instruction is for making one favor at a time. Using the assembly line process will enable you to make ten favors in less than ten times the time stated.)

Start with a clean, clutter-free workspace, and make sure everything you are working with is clean and ready to go. If you are decorating glass votive holders, for example, make sure you have washed each one thoroughly with detergent and warm water and given the glass ample time to dry. Glue always works best on a clean, dust and dirt-free surface.

The following is a list of supplies and tools you will most likely be using, along with some tips and guidance on their use. Most of these items are available at art supply stores, party and craft suppliers, fine stationery shops, fabric shops, and discount stores.

Tape—When the instructions call for tape, unless otherwise noted, a super sticky, double-sided craft tape has been used, not the double-sided tape you buy at an office supply store.

Brushes—Most often the glue or paint has been applied with a small craft paint brush or a small sponge tip "brush".

Scissors—You will need good fabric scissors, a tougher pair for cutting heavier materials such as paper and wire stems, and a tiny set of thread or embroidery scissors for delicate work.

Glue—The projects in this book use a wide variety of glues depending upon the type of materials being joined. Super Glue, matte finish, decoupage glue, and a thick clear drying craft paste have all been used. Hot glue guns are an indispensable addition to your tools. Opt for the low temperature variety in order to cut down on burnt fingertips.

Rulers—You will find a need for both a straight edge ruler or yardstick and a soft, cloth tape measure that can be wrapped around items for measuring.

Sewing—All of the projects in the book that call for sewing can also be hot glued, so if you don't have a sewing machine, don't worry. You will be able to use a thin strip of hot glue instead. Keep in mind it is best if you work with a strip of hot glue no longer than about three inches in order to keep it from hardening before you've used it. Hot glue dries very quickly.

Stuffing—The favors in the book were stuffed with either dacron batting or dried floral potpourri, depending upon the desired textures. If you opt for batting, it is important to mix the scented potpourri oil into the batting BEFORE you stuff it into the sachet so that the oil will not stain the fabric.

Potpourri Scented Batting Recipe

Use 6 drops of scented potpourri oil for 16 oz. of batting. In a separate bag, mix the oil and batting, using your hands to thoroughly and evenly mix the oil into the Dacron. Transfer the required amount of scented stuffing into your sachet.

Matte Sealer—Many of the projects call for a matte sealer to be applied. You can substitute Aqua Net aerosol hair spray for the sealer in all recipes. Note: Do not use matte sealer on votive holders or candles as it is flammable.

Placecard Note—It is easier to print the names of your guests on the card inserts and insert them into the frame first, *before* decorating the frame. You can use a butter knife to pry open stubborn frames.

Measuring—The importance of accurate measuring cannot be stressed strongly enough. Always measure before cutting and if in doubt, leave a little extra. The measurements quoted in this book will fit the components we used. The materials you purchase may be sized slightly different, so it is important to confirm measurements before you begin.

Ribbon Looping

A technique widely used throughout the book is looping a ribbon instead of tying it in a bow. To make a double loop: Take the piece of ribbon and make a fold at 4" (or whatever measurement stated in the instructions) from the bottom length of the ribbon. Loop the fold down about 1¾", then bring ribbon up again. Form another loop right in front of the first loop but about ¼" smaller. Both ends should dangle and be about the same length with only ¼" or so inches difference in size. If you were to look at the ribbon sideways, it would look like a capital M with the second hump slightly shorter than the first. For the triple loop, see drawing, below.

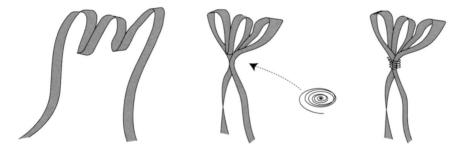

Our Rating System

A dollar sign ($) has been assigned for every two dollars of cost associated with the favors. This only includes the ingredients listed on the materials list, so if candy is listed, then it is included in the cost. Otherwise, costs are without the candy needed to fill the favor.

Please note that all prices are estimates only. Cost and availability will vary.

At the end of each section we've listed the purchased favors and their approximate suggested retail prices by page number.

Bridal Table

Jack + Myr

...re the joy of our marriage
...day, the fourth of December
...n hundred ninety three
...ne o'clock in the afternoon

Teresa B. Rankin

WEDDING FAVORS

O F ALL OUR CELEBRATIONS, surely weddings are the crown jewel. And rightfully so. Weddings symbolize the union of two people, the uniqueness of their bond, and their desire to share it with friends and family. Weddings are a symbol of hope, of memories shared and commitments witnessed. This is the one time we are not afraid to be extravagant, realizing that quality stands out and is unmistakable. Certainly, the favors used for a wedding can reflect the mood of the whole affair.

At formal weddings, guests spend much of their time at the table so using your favor ideas to create a wonderful impression is time well spent. Elegantly executed food, such as chocolate sculptures or elaborately decorated cookies or mini cakes, can make wonderful favors. Placecards can be as effortless as a stunning silver frame or as elaborate as a hand-crafted placecard that comes close to being a work of art.

Many brides will delight in shopping for the perfect token of their appreciation, while others eagerly look forward to personally making special favors for their guests to take home. Consider throwing a favor making party with laughter, food, drink, and lots of women having fun together while creating beautiful things.

Whatever method you choose, you'll find the following pages filled with unique embellishments for your wedding table.

A SILVER AND WHITE WEDDING

The clean, simple beauty of white is accented with just a touch of silver or platinum. From the ease of purchased silver frames for your guests, to the more personalized delicate silver leaf placecards gracing your table, there are an abundance of choices to fit all budgets, time schedules, and skill levels. Votives, whether hand decorated like these shown or left unadorned, are a beautiful way to add warmth and sparkle to any reception table.

Candies have always been a wedding favor staple. Chocolate is certainly the sweet most associated with love and romance and is always appropriate for weddings, in any of its forms. Truffles can be showcased in an elegant silver coaster and decorated with tulle, flowers, and ribbons. Smaller chocolates can be held in small, paper handbags, or tiny organza bags, which can be used 'as is', or to which you can add a personalized, decorative touch. Or you might consider candy-coated almonds, which are often used to symbolize both the "bitter and the sweet" of matrimonial life. For people with lots of time or a particularly handicraft bent, elegant silver sachets can grace each guest's place for a truly memorable favor.

Wedding Truffle Tray

1 Silver coaster
13″ Diameter circle of tulle
20″ Length of ⅝″ satin edged organza ribbon
20″ Length of silver cord
19″ Length of silver cord
1″ Diameter silk flower
2″ White cloth covered wire
Three chocolate truffles

Cut a 13″ circle from the tulle.

Lay flat, then place coaster on top of the tulle circle, making sure it is centered.

Place the three truffles on the coaster.

Gather the tulle up over the truffles and twist to gather. Hold the gather in place with the 2″ wire.

Holding both lengths of silver cord, wrap twice around the gathered tulle, then tie once to hold (Do not tie into a bow yet!).

Tie ribbon around the gathered tulle, directly on top of silver cording. When knotting the ribbon, make sure to loop one "tail" of the silver cording through the ribbon in order to merge the two together.

Holding all three pieces (both cord lengths and the length of ribbon), tie into a bow. Adjust the lengths.

Knot the end of the cording and trim the edge of the ribbon.

Hot glue flower onto the knot of the bow.

Time: 4 minutes   **Skill Level: Beginner**   **Cost: $$$**

White Rosette & Ribbon Organza Bag

White organza bag measuring 3″ across and 5″ long
White organza poinsettia with pearl center, 2″ wide
   (or other flower of your choice)
12″ White taffeta ribbon, ⅞″ wide
11″ Thin silver cording
Hot glue

Take the 12″ piece of taffeta ribbon and make a fold at 4″ from the bottom length of the ribbon. Loop the fold down about 1¾″, then bring ribbon up again. Form another loop right in front of the first loop but about ¼″ smaller. Both ends should dangle and be about the same length with only ¼″ or so difference in size. If you were to look at the ribbon sideways, it would look like a capital M with the second hump slightly shorter than the first.

Take the silver cord and, about 3″ from the left edge, begin wrapping around the double looped ribbon, making sure to catch the 1¾″ middle loop. Wrap the cording around the ribbon loops three times, then tie once in the back.

Hot glue the ribbon cluster on the top left of the organza bag, right below the drawstring line, being careful not to catch the draw cord with the glue. When gluing, tilt the ribbon cluster at about a 45 degree angle.

Knot cords at ends and trim the ribbon edges at an angle.

Hot glue the flower right on top of the silver cord cluster.

Time: 4 minutes   Skill Level: Beginner   Cost: $$

Leaf Placecard

1 Silver-edged fold-over tent style placecard 3½″ x 4″ (folds to 2″ x 3½″)

1 Silver leaf (sold in fabric and craft shops)

Clear-drying scrapbook paste

Small craft brush or sponge

Fold the placecard in half and place in front of you. Select a leaf and brush with glue. Place on card with stem end about ¼″ – ⅜″ from bottom right hand corner. Lay across card at an angle with the tip of the leaf going slightly beyond the top edge of the card. The edge of the leaf should cross the top of the card at about ⅜″ – ½″ from the upper top left corner. Each leaf will be slightly different in size and shape so this will be a judgment call. You may write the names first and then place the leaves over them, or write the names directly on top of the leaf, being careful not to pull or tug.

Time: 2 minutes   Skill Level: Beginner   Cost: $

Pearl Trimmed Votive Holder

Glass votive cup with flared lip, 2″ high

8½″ length white pearl trim

Tea Light candle

Super Glue or Krazy Glue

Make sure votive cup is clean before starting. Apply thin strip of glue along bead trim. Press into place along upper lip of glass votive.

Time: 2 minutes

Skill Level: Beginner

Cost: $

Silver Sachet

Antique satin in light silver, 5″ x 5½″
5½″ Embroidered organza ribbon in white and gray, 3½″ wide
13″ White organza ribbon with silver edge, 1″ wide
Beaded flower in white, approximately 1″ wide
4″ Thin wire
¾ Cup of scented dacron stuffing (see page 16)

NOTE: All seam allowances are ¼".

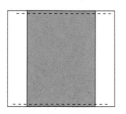

Center the ribbon on the right side of the satin. Stitch into place along seam allowances.

Fold right sides of fabric (the side with the ribbon) together and stitch across ends leaving 1" open in the middle.

Position stitched fabric so that seam runs down the center, facing you. Stitch side seams.

Turn pillow right side out through the one inch opening. Stuff with scented filling.

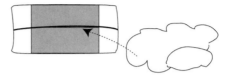

Glue 1" opening closed using hot glue gun.

Fold the 1" wide white organza ribbon with silver edges into three loops approximately 1" high each. Front and back tails should be approximately 2½" long. Secure loops in place with tie wire or dab of hot glue.

Using a dab of hot glue, affix loops on sachet at top right hand corner at an angle. Trim ribbon at an angle. Using another dab of hot glue, glue beaded flower into place, pressing the ribbon ends up and under flower to cover wire.

Time: 12 minutes   Skill Level: Intermediate   Cost: $$

ELEGANT TRADITIONS

Nothing says bridal like the classic elegance of white. For a stylish, traditional celebration, you might consider adding beautiful white ribbons or floral embellishments to a striking silver wedding bell. The white trim on the flowerpot votive holders picks up the white color theme, adding a warm radiance to the table. Guests will love taking home sweets, like the chocolate kisses shown here, or use white candy coated almonds to play up the white theme.

Bridal Bells

1 Silverplated wedding bell
18″ Embroidered white organza ribbon, 1½″ wide

Tie ribbon around bell handle, just above the bell.
Trim edges in W shape

1 Silverplated wedding bell
White flower cluster with pearl center,
  1¼″ wide
18″ White satin rimmed organza ribbon, ⅝″ wide
Hot glue

   Tie ribbon around bell handle as in above
instructions. Hot glue flower onto the middle of the
bow.

Time: 2 minutes   Skill Level: Beginner   Cost: $$$

Flowerpot Votive Holders

1 Glass flowerpot style votive,
  either clear or frosted, 2¾″ high
10″ Ribbon or trim, ¾″ to 1″ wide
Super Glue or Krazy Glue
White votive candle

Measure the rim of the votive cup
to confirm measurement. Apply glue to
trim, press against top edge of glass
votive. Fill with candle.

Time: 2 minutes   Skill Level: Beginner   Cost: $$

White Feathered Cord Organza Bag

White organza bag measuring 3″ across and 5″ long
3 Small white porcelain flowers (about ½″ long) on wire stem
2 6″ Lengths of white satin ribbon, ¹⁄₁₆″ wide
3 5″ Lengths of white feathered cording
Hot glue

Take all five strips and lay them together. Knot once in the middle. Using the hot glue, affix the knotted ribbon cluster onto the center of the organza bag, right below the drawstring. Drape both sides down. Press three flower cluster into the wet glue, and bring ends of ribbon and cording up to cover the wire stem ends. Pinch to secure the ribbons in the glue.

Time: 3 minutes   **Skill Level: Beginner**   **Cost: $$**

AN ELEGANT GOLD AND IVORY WEDDING

There is something about gold that communicates sumptuousness. Furthermore, the richness of the color works equally well with either ivory or white.

With gold it is important not to overwhelm, but to accent. Delicate gold braiding accents one of the picture frame placecards, and the vellum covered votive holder. Pick up the gold theme in the Florentine pattern on the favor pyramid box and the gold covered chocolates in the organza bag. Just the merest hint of gold enhances the scrollwork on the blue and cream covered votive holder, and the pearl encrusted topiary is gently sponged with the softest of gold washes. The idea here is to apply the slightest touch of gold in order to add to the richness of the occasion.

Gold Cord Draped Placecard

Ivory Pictureframe Placecard
36″ Gold cording
Hot glue

Cut cording into two 16" strips and one 4" strip. Laying the two 16" strips together, tie a bow. Knot all four ends. Put a dab of hot glue on the upper left hand corner of the Pictureframe Placecard. Press the knot of the bow into the dab of glue. Drape ends up and around the top of the frame, placing a dab of glue to hold in place, then again where the one cord crosses over the other. Do the same with the ends of the bow that trail down the left hand side of the frame.

Loop the 4" piece of cord into a double loop. Position loops on the bottom right hand corner. Turn frame over and hot glue the loops into place on the back side.

Time: 2 minutes   Skill Level: Beginner   Cost: $

Gold Scrolled Corners Placecard

Ivory Pictureframe Placecard
2 Gold tone scroll-work metal corners (from craft stores)
Linen colored acrylic paint
Hot glue
Small sponge brush (optional)

Hot glue gold corners into place. With fingers or sponging brush, wipe linen colored acrylic paint over gold scrollwork, making sure to push paint up into creases for a patina-like look. Before paint dries, polish with paper towel to remove excess.

Time: 4 minutes   Skill Level: Beginner   Cost: $$

Ivory Flowers Organza Bag

Ivory organza bag measuring 3″ across and 5″ long
3 Small (1″ in diameter) ivory organza flowers
2 Pieces 7″ Ivory satin ribbon, ¼″ wide
Hot glue

Take the two pieces of 7" ribbon and and loop once. This will make a two-loop cluster, one on top of the other. Using a dab of hot glue, affix ribbons to organza bag right below drawstring, at an angle. Using another dab of hot glue for each flower, secure flowers onto organza bag.

Time: 4 minutes   **Skill Level: Beginner**   **Cost: $$**

Pearl Topiary

1 Small terra cotta flowerpot, 2″ high
2″ Diameter Styrofoam ball
6″ Green floral stick or wooden dowel ¼ – ⅜″ in diameter
Green florist foam
Sea foam moss (available at craft stores)
2 Pieces of gold cording, 22″ each
12″ Satin ribbon in white or ivory, ½″ wide
¼ Cup of mixed size ivory craft pearl beads
Thick clear-drying scrapbook paste
Double-sided sticky tape
Spray crackle medium
Gold acrylic paint
Linen acrylic paint
Sponge applicator
Hot glue

Apply gold paint to flowerpot using sponge applicator. Let dry. Apply crackle medium to the area below the rim of the flowerpot. Follow manufacturer's instructions, and while still tacky, apply a thin coat of linen colored acrylic paint using a smearing technique. As the paint dries, the crackle finish will emerge.

Fill pot with green florist foam. Apply hot glue to the top of the foam and hand press sea foam moss into the glue, allowing the moss to tumble over the edge of the flowerpot for a natural effect.

Cover dowel with double-sided sticky tape, then starting at the top, place the ribbon at an angle and wrap the entire dowel with the ribbon, making sure to overlap edges in order to completely cover the stick. Press stick into foam. Press Styrofoam ball onto top of dowel. Apply craft paste to entire Styrofoam ball with fingers. Put pearls into paper plate, then turn the topiary structure upside down and press the sticky Styrofoam ball into pearl mixture. Completely cover the ball, using your fingers, if necessary, to press pearls into the harder-to-reach areas. Using hand, firmly press all pearls into the paste in order to adhere firmly.

Take a piece of cording. Leave a 4" tail and form a double figure-eight. Pinch between your fingers and place a dab of hot glue to secure. This should leave another 4" tail on the other side. Apply dab of hot glue onto bottom of pearl sphere where it joins the stick. Push gold cord figure-eight loops into this glue to adhere. Repeat on the other side. Knot ends of cord.

Time: 30 minutes   **Skill Level: Advanced**   **Cost: $$**

Wrapping Paper Votive

1 Glass votive cup, 2″ in diameter and 2½″ high

Wrapping paper, 2½″ wide by 7¼″ long, cut straight or with deckled edge

22" Sheer white organza ribbon with gold edge, ½″ wide

Votive candle

Super sticky double-sided craft tape

Wrap paper around glass votive, affixing in back with special craft quality super sticky double-faced tape. Wrap gold ribbon around votive, tying in a bow in the front. Trim ends. Place candle in cup.

Time: 3 minutes   Skill Level: Beginner   Cost: $$

Vellum Wrapped Votive

Glass votive cup, 2″ in diameter and 2½″ high

Vellum, 2½″ wide by 7¼″ long, cut straight or with deckled edge

22″ Gold cord

Votive candle

Super sticky double-sided craft tape

Wrap vellum around glass votive, affixing in back with special craft quality super sticky double-faced tape. Wrap the gold cording around the votive twice, beginning and ending in the front. Tie a knot, then knot both ends to finish off cording and keep from fraying. Place candle in cup.

Time: 3 minutes   Skill Level: Beginner   Cost: $$

WEDDING POSIES

Not all weddings are formal affairs and some will definitely lend themselves to the charm of a small tin bucket filled with white candy coated almonds or a single hyacinth bloom. A miniature tin watering can makes a perfect accent for a garden wedding and can hold a small white votive candle or delicate lily of the valley. Any wedding, regardless of its degree of formality, will enjoy small individual glass vases filled with whatever flower suits your fancy.

SIMPLE WEDDING FAVORS

Wedding favors don't need to be fancy in order to be striking. A miniature white brocade covered book tied with a ribbon makes an unusual, but very simple wedding favor. A small white porcelain box accented with gold or silver and filled with the confection of your choice is another easy option. The delicate glow from personalized votives always adds to the air of romance and intimacy.

Pearly Votive

Glass votive cup, 2″ in diameter and 2½″ high
89″ String of tiny pearl trim
Hot glue
White votive candle

Beginning at bottom edge, anchor a row of pearls using the hot glue. Be careful not to work too far ahead or the glue will harden before you've used it. As you continue to wrap rows of pearl beads, use an occasional dab of hot glue to anchor in place. End pearl trim at center back. Run a seam of hot glue up the back to anchor each row.

    Time: 6 minutes   **Skill Level: Beginner**   **Cost: $$**

Vellum "Collar" Votive

Glass votive cup, 2″ in diameter and 2½″ high
Vellum, 2½″ wide by 7¼″ long, cut with deckled edge
Two small (¼″ diameter) white flowers
Votive candle
Super sticky double-sided craft tape
Super Glue or Krazy Glue

Apply super sticky double-sided tape to front of votive holder, one inch down from the top edge. Wrap vellum around glass votive so that it meets in the front, and press it into the double-faced tape. The top inch will remain loose. Fold the two top edges down, like a shirt collar. Using Super Glue, affix two small flowers in place along front vellum "seam". Place candle in cup.

    Time: 3 minutes   **Skill Level: Beginner**   **Cost: $$**

A UNIQUE WEDDING

One of the wonderful things about evolving wedding trends is the increasing adventurousness of today's brides They arc unafraid to go all out in their quest for a unique wedding. These weddings are planned as a personal statement, infused with the bride's own wonderful sense of style. The hint of a feather or two, a string of shimmering rhinestones, or the well-planned placement of large crystals can turn a plain glass votive into a work of art. Traditional organza bags can be dressed up with all-out finery, while glitter and jewels enhance Pictureframe Placecards. For a truly all-out touch, surprise your guests with a wild and wonderful feather topiary, or an extravagant silver and pearl sachet purse.

Full of sparkle, zest, and *joie de vivre*, these type of weddings are always an event to be remembered.

Feather and Bead Placecard

1 Silver matte Pictureframe Placecard
4″ Strand of feathered cord
Mixture of colorful beads in complimentary colors
   and varying shapes and sizes
   (for this frame we used small dark blue and
   purple round beads, a large clear crystal bead, and
   a few "rice" shaped silver beads)
Thick clear-drying scrapbook paste

Apply a penny-size dab of paste about ¼" thick to the top left corner of frame. Press feathered cord into the glue in a random pattern with approximately 1" sticking out above the frame and about another two inches dangling down the left side of the frame. Sprinkle a large pinch of the beading mixture into the paste, then press down firmly to make sure it adheres thoroughly, moving the beads around in the paste until the desired effect is achieved.

Time: 3 minutes   Skill Level: Beginner   Cost: $$

Feather Votive Holder

Clear glass flowerpot style votive holder
5 Small white craft feathers, about 3 – 4″ each
1 Small white craft feather with bead on the
   quill, 4″ long
3″ Silver feather cord
3″ Magenta feather cord
Mixture of colorful beads in complementary
   colors and varying shapes and sizes
Thick clear-drying scrapbook paste
Votive candle

Place a dime-size dab of paste in the center of the votive holder right below the lip of the flowerpot. Place the feathers and cord into the paste, fluffing out and spacing to desired effect. Sprinkle beads onto the paste, then push firmly to anchor it all.

Time: 4 minutes   Skill Level: Beginner   Cost: $$

Rhinestone Votive Holder

Glass votive cup, 2″ in diameter and 2½″ high
22″ String of rhinestones (from craft or fabric store)
Super or Krazy Glue
Votive candle

Beginning in the back, anchor the strand of rhinestones at the top of the votive with the glue. (You may prefer to apply glue to the entire rhinestone strand for extra security—just be careful not to get any on your fingers.) Wind the rhinestone string around the cup three times, ending up in the back. Secure the last end with glue.

Time: 4 minutes   **Skill Level: Beginner**   **Cost: $$**

Crystal Decorated Votive Holder

Glass votive cup, 2″ in diameter and 2½″ high
5 Large square decorative crystals approx. ⅞″
  (available in craft or fabric store)
5 Small rectangular decorative crystals approx. ⅜″
Super or Krazy Glue
Votive candle

Apply glue to the backside of a crystal. You will need to hold each crystal in place for a few seconds so that it doesn't slip back off. Apply the large square crystals evenly spaced on the bottom row, tilted at a 45 degree angle so that it is "diamond" shaped. In the spaces between the larger crystals, apply the smaller rectangular crystals "lengthwise", also evenly spaced.

Time: 4 minutes   **Skill Level: Beginner**   **Cost: $$**

Feather Topiary

1 Clear glass flowerpot style votive holder, 2¾″ high
2″ Diameter Styrofoam ball
6″ Green floral stick or wooden dowel ¼″ – ⅜″ in diameter
Green florist foam
12″ Circle of light lilac tulle
½ Cup dried Spanish moss, spray painted white
18 White craft feathers with 1½″ stem with two beads attached
7″ Double-sided sticky tape
2 White craft feathers snipped into ¼″ pieces of fluff
Bead mixture
Pearlescent spray paint in violet
Thick clear-drying scrapbook paste
Embroidery needle

Spray paint the flowerpot with the violet paint, using a light, misting motion. Turn upside down to dry. Should dry for at least 30 min. Mold florist foam into the shape of the container, using your hands. Cover the molded foam with the painted Spanish moss. Place in the center of the 12" circle of tulle. Gather tulle up and stuff the entire wad into the flowerpot. Trim and fluff tulle so that it sticks up approximately 1½" beyond rim of flowerpot, forming a ruffle.

Cover stick with double-sided sticky tape. Sprinkle bead mixture onto dowel, pushing smaller beads into the tape with your fingers. Leave bottom two inches clear of beads as well as the top inch. Press Styrofoam ball onto top of dowel pushing down about an inch. Using finger, cover entire ball with craft paste. Then randomly sprinkle beads and snipped feathers onto the paste. Using hands, press firmly into place. Using leftover tulle trimmings and a large embroidery needle, push the tiny tulle trimmings into the ball to anchor it, going about ¼" deep in nine random places evenly spaced around the ball. They will look like little tulle "tufts". Using the same embroidery needle, pierce a hole, then insert one of the 18" long-stemmed craft feathers. Do this 17 more times, randomly spacing feathers around the sphere to create a palm tree effect. Be careful while guiding feathers into the holes, so as not to bend the stem or the feather will look droopy.

Time: 30 minutes   **Skill Level: Advanced**   **Cost: $$$**

Feather and Silver Net Organza Bag

Lilac organza bag, measuring 3″ across and 5″ long
3 White craft feathers, 2½″ – 3″ long
3 8″ Lengths white satin ribbon, ¹⁄₁₆″ wide
2 Pieces soft silver mesh fabric or ribbon, 3″ x 2″

Pinch feathers, two up and one down, between fingers. Wrap silver mesh around feathers at center, tie with the three strands of ¹⁄₁₆" ribbon. Wrap center of ribbon around center of feathers and knot off. Fluff mesh ends to look like a pinwheel. Trim ends of ribbon.

Time: 3 minutes   Skill Level: Beginner   Cost: $$

Glitterati Placecard

Silver Matte Pictureframe Placecard
Fine clear, iridescent crystal glitter
Matte finish decoupage glue
Small craft brush or sponge

With the small brush, apply matte finish decoupage glue to the entire frame. Sprinkle the fine iridescent crystal glitter all over, making sure to cover all parts of the frame. Allow to dry for a few minutes, then shake off the excess. The iridescent glitter catches the light and acquires a purple-ish tint to it. (You might want to put down a piece of wax paper to catch all the extra glitter.)

Time: 2 minutes   **Skill Level: Beginner**   **Cost: $**

VINTAGE KEEPSAKES

Perhaps because of the romantic traditions surrounding weddings, we often find ourselves interested in incorporating vintage elements in our nuptial celebrations. Whether it's a bit of antique lace, our grandmother's gloves, or a Victorian style reception, a touch of the past often finds its way into the celebration of our future. Vintage keepsakes your guests are sure to treasure include placecards decorated to capture the feel of a cherished heirloom and a stylish votive candle holder with dangling crystals.

Vintage Floral Placecard (top)

1 Ivory Pictureframe Placecard
3 Blush and mocha satin applique rosettes with pearl accents
3″ Sheer organza ribbon in light mocha color, ⁷⁄₁₆″ wide

These type of satin appliques are usually sold by the yard so you'll need to cut the rosettes out with a pair of tiny thread or embroidery scissors. Hot glue two of them side by side in the top left hand corner. Take the 3″ of light mocha ribbon and wrap it around two fingers twice, so that you form two loops on each side. Hot glue the ribbon onto the bottom left hand corner of the frame. Hot glue the last rosette in the center of the ribbon.

Time: 4 minutes   **Skill Level: Beginner**   **Cost: $$**

Vintage Trim Placecard (bottom right)

1 White Pictureframe Placecard
5¼″ of ½″ – ¾″ wide decorative trim
Hot glue

Slightly pry the backing from the frame in the two upper corners. With a dab of hot glue, affix one end of the trim to the back of the frame by hot gluing it under the backing about ¼". Place a few dabs of hot glue along back of trim and press into place along the top of the frame. Finish by gluing the final end of the trim under the opposite corner, behind the backing. Quickly press backing into the still wet hot glue to re-seal.

Time: 2 minutes   **Skill Level: Beginner**   **Cost: $$**

Vintage Ribbon Wreath Placecard (page 48)

1 Ivory Pictureframe Placecard
2 Pieces 24″ Sheer organza ribbon in ivory and light mocha, ⁷⁄₁₆″ wide
5 Ivory porcelain Calla lillies, about ¾″ long (trim wire stems to ⅛″)
Hot glue

Hot glue Calla lillies onto frame, placing them at 10:00, 12:00, 2:00 4:00 and 6:00 positions around the oval opening. Take both pieces of the ribbon and, holding them loosely together, weave them around the frame opening affixing them at each porcelain flower to hide the "stem". Leave the ribbon loose and twist it slightly for a random, flowing effect. Finish off with a series of loops, press into glue, then trim ends.

Time: 5 minutes   Skill Level: Intermediate   Cost: $$

Vintage Keepsake Goblet

Glass goblet style votive holder (4″ tall, 2¾″ diameter at the top)
10″ Trim with 1¾″ – 2¼″ long bead dangles
Hot glue
Votive candle

Working only a few inches at a time, affix beaded trimming to the lip of the votive cup with the hot glue. When dry, add votive candle.

Time: 3 minutes   Skill Level: Beginner   Cost: $$

Purchased Wedding Favors Listing

SHOWERS, TEAS, AND LUNCHEONS

THERE ARE SOME OCCASIONS that are particularly and enduringly feminine. Certainly teas, girls-only showers, and women's luncheons fall into this category. These are the celebrations where we indulge in all things female: lace, ornate silver, flowers, pastel colors, tiny but beautifully presented finger food, and luscious dessert treats. We carefully iron our antique lace linens, polish our grandmother's tea set, and put out our finest, most delicate table decorations.

We have presented a wide variety of favor ideas in this section. Lavender sachets made from delicate antique handkerchiefs, beautiful soaps wrapped with a wisp of iridescent ribbon, and lovely, feminine sachets. In addition to their role as favors, many of the ideas presented in this section also make lovely attendant or hostess gifts. What better way to show your appreciation to your bridesmaids than by a lovely handmade gift? What hostess wouldn't welcome one of these lovely items into her home? Additionally, some of the topiaries featured in this section would lend themselves to particularly stunning centerpieces, at weddings or other occasions.

"PRETTY IN PINK" TEA

There is really nothing quite as romantically feminine as a Victorian Tea Party. Here we can indulge in all the female antique lace and ornate silver fantasies that tend to give our male counterparts a bad case of the fidgets. Pink organza ribbons, white lace, fancy silver teapots, bone china tea cups, and pastel flower arrangements — nothing is too over the top for this kind of occasion.

Teas lend themselves particularly well to charming and effortless entertaining due to the make-ahead nature of the refreshments served. It creates an ideal setting for a low-key, relaxed shower. Indulge your guests with beautifully hand made sachets, filled with your favorite delicate scent. Pretty placecards can help your guests find their seats. And what woman can resist a delicately cut perfume bottle or a prettily decorated, sweet-smelling soap? Accent your table with delicate little tea lights, enhanced with pink bead trim or crystals. Or take the color scheme in fresh directions with a charming rice-paper-wrapped votive holder accented with a pink silk ribbon and wax seal. Whatever favors you choose, take the opportunity to add romance and feminine appeal to every aspect of your celebration.

Pretty Corner Sachet Pockets

10″ square fabric
10″ square inexpensive sheer fabric
¾ Cup dried flower potpourri
Hot glue
16″ Sheer organza ribbon in dark rose, ⅝″
Organza flower

Cut 10" square of fabric Place on table with wrong side up.

Fold all edges over ¼", press, then use hot glue to glue them in place.

Cut 10" piece of inexpensive, sheer fabric.

Lay flat on table, wrong side up and fill with ¾ cup of pretty dried flower potpourri.

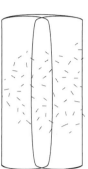

Fold both sides to middle, overlapping about 1 – 2".

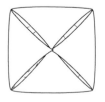

Repeat with top and bottom to form a wrapped packet of about 3 – 3½". Hot glue packet closed.

Place sheer packet fold side down in the center of the finished edge fabric from step one. Finished edge fabric should be wrong side up, and packet should sit on the wrong side.

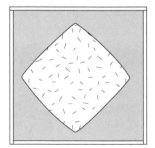

Place a dab of hot glue smaller than a dime onto the center of the sheer packet. Bring four corners of outside fabric into the middle.

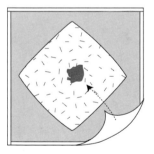

Press each of the four corners into the hot glue. Fabric should sink down into center glue spot.

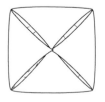

Using the hot glue, affix the deep rose ribbon, then glue the organza flowers on top of that.

Time: 10–12 minutes   **Skill Level: Intermediate**   **Cost: $–$$**

Square Doily Sachet with Woven Ribbon

2 Square fabric doilies, 5″ square (purchased at fabric or craft stores)
32″ Sheer organza ribbon in deep rose, ½″ wide
2 Small heart charms with "eye" on top for hanging
2 3″ Lengths white satin ribbon, ¹⁄₁₆″ wide
½ Cup dacron stuffing (see page 16)
Hot glue

Apply hot glue along all edges of square, leaving a 1½″ wide opening for stuffing.

Press second doily (wrong side down) into the warm glue.

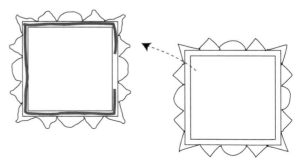

TIP: It is easier and it looks smoother if you leave the opening along one of the straight edges instead of leaving the opening at a corner.

After glue dries, insert stuffing into square. Use a small blunt object (like the eraser edge of a pencil or a small dowel) to push stuffing into the points of the square.

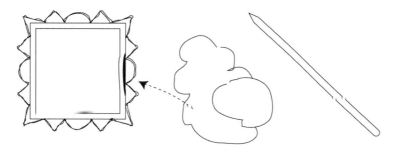

Glue opening shut, making sure not to catch any stuffing in the seam.

Fold 32" piece of dark rose ribbon in half. The halfway mark is your starting point, you will be weaving one half of the ribbon in one direction and the other half in the opposite direction.

Weave the ribbon to the right going in and out of openings along the lace doily edges, until you reach the corner opposite from where you started.

Return to the starting point, and repeat this process, this time weaving the ribbon to the left until both ends meet at the far corner. NOTE: Do not pull ribbon taught as you want a loosely woven effect. Also, twist the ribbon slightly to give it a sense of movement.

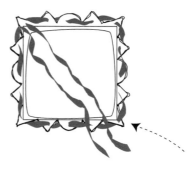

Tie one of the tiny heart charms onto each of the $1/16$" wide satin ribbon, knotting the ribbon just above the charm so that it is held in place.

Using hot glue, just below the deep rose bow, glue all four ends of the two charm ribbons into place making sure to stagger the placement so the charms do not hang evenly.

Hot glue deep rose bow over the ribbon ends to cover.

Time: 10 minutes   **Skill Level: Beginner**   **Cost: $–$$**

Dried Floral Placecard

Ivory Pictureframe Placecard
Dried flowers and leaves
Decoupage glue
Matte sealer
Paintbrush or sponge applicator

Apply decoupage glue to the back of the dried flowers. Apply flowers to top left corner of frame and bottom right corner of frame. Bring flowers out slightly along the sides for a more continuous look. Brush matte sealer on top of dried flowers to seal. Finish with decoupage glue.

Time: 2 minutes   **Skill Level: Beginner**   **Cost: $**

Gold and Pink Beaded Placecard

Matte gold Pictureframe Placecard
Double-sided super sticky tape
Small, opalescent pink beads
Micro gold beads
Matte sealer

Apply a strip of the super sticky double-sided tape all along the outside rim of the frame.

Snip extra bits of the tape to fill in at the corners for a more rounded effect. Press the beads onto the tape. Spray with matte sealer.

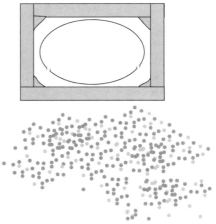

Time: 3 minutes
Skill Level: Beginner
Cost: $

Pink Pearl Placecard

Ivory Pictureframe Placecard
8″ Pink pearls on string or wire
Krazy or Super Glue

Starting just to the right of the center of the oval opening, glue pearls along opening, right along edge.

Time: 2 minutes   **Skill Level: Beginner**   **Cost: $**

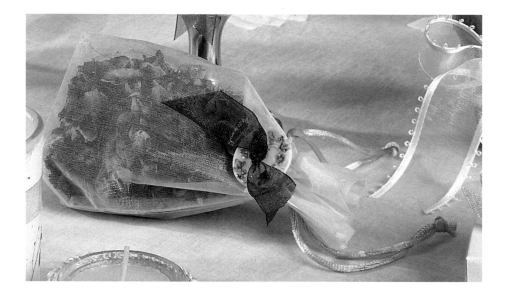

Rose Porcelain Button Organza Bag

Pink organza bag, measuring 3″ across and 5″ long
1 Handpainted, porcelain button measuring 1″ in diameter
4″ Sheer organza ribbon in burgundy, ½″ wide
¼ Cup dried rose petals or rose petal potpourri
Hot glue

Thread ribbon through porcelain button. Knot it to secure. Trim ribbon edges at an angle. Hot glue button in center of organza bag, directly below drawstring line. Fill with petals.

Time: 3 minutes   **Skill Level: Beginner**   **Cost: $$**

White Paper Wrapped Votive Holder

Glass votive cup, 2″ in diameter and 2½″ high
White rice paper with tiny botanical elements, 2½″ wide by 7¼″ long,
   cut with deckled edge
14″ Pink silk ribbon, ½″ wide
Sealing wax in white
Seal
Super or Krazy Glue
Hot glue
Decoupage glue
Votive candle

Lay cut rice paper on table in front of you with RIGHT side down.
Apply decoupage glue to the wrong side of the paper. Place the glass votive
in the center of the glued paper and bring ends up to wrap and cover the
glass holder completely. Wrap pink silk ribbon around center, holding in
place with a dab of Super Glue. Make wax seal on a piece of wax paper,
then transfer to ribbon, affixing it with a dab of hot glue.

Time: 5 minutes   **Skill Level: Beginner**   **Cost: $$**

Beaded Bowl-Style Votive Holder

Glass bowl-style votive holder, 2½″ x 2½″
Masking tape, 1″ wide
Mixed bead assortment (we used tiny gold, pearlescent pink and mini fuschia beads)
Thick clear-drying scrapbook paste
Votive candle
Decoupage glue to seal
Small sponge tip applicator

Carefully apply six strips of the tape along the sides of the votive holder lengthwise. This will keep the beads from getting into this area. Make sure to lay down the tape as straight as possible. Apply scrapbook paste glue on the exposed area. Sprinkle beads onto the glue, using fingers to press them in gently. Let dry. Remove tape. Brush a thin coat of decoupage glue over the beads to seal.

Time: 5 minutes   Skill Level: Beginner   Cost: $$

Pink Decoupage Flowerpot Votive Holder

Glass flowerpot-style votive holder, 2¾″ high
27″ of white, organza ribbon with looped edge, 1″ wide
Tissue paper, approximately 8″ x 11″
White votive candle
Hot glue

Tear tissue paper into small 2″ pieces. Cover the back of each piece with decoupage glue and randomly apply glue side to the glass flowerpot. Make sure to overlay the pieces and completely cover the glass. Apply one coat of decoupage glue over the entire paper-covered glass to seal.

After cup dries, hot glue the center of the 27″ piece of ribbon to back of flowerpot. Bring ribbon around to the front and tie a bow and trim ends.

Time: 7 minutes   **Skill Level: Beginner**   **Cost: $$**

PEACHY BRIDESMAIDS' LUNCHEON

Peach is another delicious pastel shade that appeals to our romantic natures. Inviting and soft, peach casts a warm, delicate glow on everything that surrounds it and is perfect for an intimate bridesmaids' luncheon or a bridal or baby shower. Little unexpected touches can reinforce a theme in a variety of wonderful ways, from delicate peach flowers on the placecards, to a fun "martini" made of peach-colored fizzing bath balls. Floral shaped and frosted glass perfume bottles keep the feeling warm and light. An elegant tablecloth, a beautifully painted tiny box, all help to set the tone of the party.

Peach Floral Wreath Placecard

Ivory Pictureframe Placecard
25 Small paper flowers in peach with green stems
Hot glue

Apply a strip of hot glue, (only work two inches at a time so hot glue doesn't dry before you're ready) along oval frame opening. Carefully place flowers along glued edge, positioning so that the blossoms all open along the same way. Tuck stems under and around surrounding flowers.

Time: 10 minutes   Skill Level: Beginner   Cost: $$–$$$

Peach Floral Cluster Placecard

Ivory Pictureframe Placecard
Floral cluster with peach flowers and greenery, approx. 4″ long and 1″ wide
Hot glue

Apply a two-inch long strip of hot glue along bottom right edge of frame, approximately ¼" from right edge. Place flower cluster into glue, arranging stems and leaves to suit. Apply a thin strip of hot glue up along right hand edge of frame, about 1½" high. Pull branches and flowers up along right hand edge, pressing into glue.

Time: 2 minutes   Skill Level: Beginner   Cost: $$

Peach Hankie Pouf

1 Square, peach colored hankie
4 17″ Lengths of ribbon, ⅛″ each wide
8″ Square of sheer chiffon
½ Cup dried botanical potpourri
Embroidery needle

Place hankie on flat surface with the wrong side facing you. Thread a large embroidery needle with one of the strands of ribbon.

From the RIGHT side of the fabric (the side laying on the table) poke a hole into the center top of the hankie. Pull the needle all the way through, then pierce a hole in the bottom center of the hankie. Repeat with the right and left sides, using a second piece of ribbon.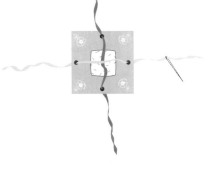

Place potpourri in a small square of sheer chiffon and glue shut. (see page 57).

Drop potpourri pouch into hankie under the ribbons.

Scooting the holes toward the center, cinch the hankie along the ribbons. Tie one set of ribbons, then the other. Fluff out the corners of the hankie, tweaking the points so that they hang nicely.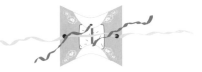

Time: 5 minutes   **Skill Level: Beginner/Intermediate**   Cost: $$

More Sachet Ideas

Sachets are such a wonderful gift, easy to make and fun to receive. Here are some more ways to make this type of favor.

Ivory Satin Stacked Sachet

1 Piece ivory satin, 11″ x 5½″
1 Piece ivory satin, 9″ x 4½″
32″ Ivory satin cord
3 Silk roses, 1½″ wide, with green leaves or stems
Scented dacron stuffing

Fold the 11" x 5½" piece of satin in half and stitch down the seam, leaving a 1" opening. Allow ½" seam allowance.

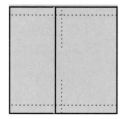

Center the seam and stitch across both of the open ends.

Turn pillow inside out through the opening. Stuff with scented dacron stuffing.

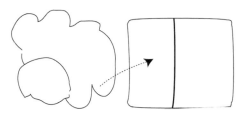

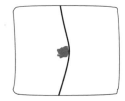

Hot glue opening closed.

Repeat process with small piece of satin to make the second pillow.

Hot glue the smaller pillow on top of the larger, making sure to center.

Wrap ivory cording around both pillows, like a present, ending with a knot on top. Hot glue the three silk roses on top of the cording.

Time: 15 minutes   Skill Level: Intermediate   Cost: $$

Lavender Silk Sachets

This sachet uses a slightly different method to make the pillows.

2 Pieces lavender raw silk, 6½″ x 4½″
2 Pieces lavender silk, 5½″ x 3¼″
1 Yard sheer organza ribbon in silver shimmer, ⅝″ wide
Hot glue
3 Silk ribbon roses, ½″ diameter
2 Green silk stems or leaves, 1½″ long
1½ Cups dried lavender
1 Cup dacron stuffing

Place the two pieces of 6½" x 4½" raw silk right sides together. Stitch up all four sides using a ½" seam allowance and leaving a 1" opening along one of the longer sides for stuffing. Turn inside out through the hole. Stuff with dried lavender. Hot glue opening closed.

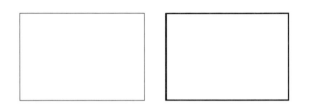

Repeat with smaller pieces of silk, but this time stuff with a combination of lavender and dacron stuffing. The dacron gives a more fluffy balanced feel to the pillow and the dried lavender will give a slightly "crunchier" feel. Glue opening closed. Stack smaller pillow on top of larger pillow.

Hot glue the the rosettes directly onto the pillow itself, then wrap with a sheer organza bow like a "present."

Time: 15 minutes   **Skill Level: Intermediate**   **Cost: $$**

Antique Linen Hankie
"Envelope" Style Sachet

1 Square hankie (Can be found at yard sales, thrift shops, antique
   stores, or swap meets)
¾ Cup potpourri or dacron stuffing
1 Small silk ribbon rosette
Hot glue

Fold square hankie in half to form a triangle.

Bring left corner into center, keeping bottom edge aligned.

Bring left point 1" past center of triangle.

Fold over the right edge in the same way, bringing the right point all the way to the left fold. Do not overlap past the edge of the hankie.

Apply thin strip of hot glue ⅛" up from the bottom edge. Press firmly and make sure no glue oozes out.

Apply another strip of hot glue along second bottom edge, press top glued fold into second strip of glue, in effect gluing all three folded edges together.

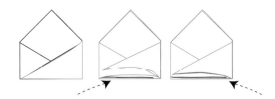

Peel apart the two layers of hankie on the top point of the "envelope." Place potpourri between the two layers, and shake down to fill so that it doesn't spill back out of the top.

Fold top over like envelope, gluing closed along V.

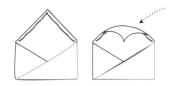

Press into place.

Hot glue silk or satin rosette into place just to the right of point.

Time: 10 minutes   Skill Level: Beginner   Cost: $–$$

(depending on cost of hankie)

Ottoman Style Sachet

2 Pieces of French wired ribbon, 2″ wide and 7″ long
1 Piece 1″ – 1¾″ ribbon, 5″ long — for middle section
2 Rosettes or other decorative embellishment

Take one of the pieces of 7" long French wire ribbon. Holding the wire edge hand gather in until the ribbon is about 6" long. From the other side, grab an end wire and gather in about an inch until the entire piece of gathered ribbon is about 5" long. You will need to do this to both sides of both pieces of ribbon.

For the best gather, you will need to gather about an inch on the top and another inch from the bottom for an evenly gathered effect.

Do not lose the wire in the ribbon.

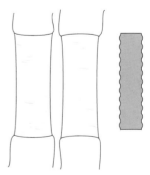

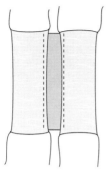

Place the 5" ribbon down with the wrong side up. Glue or sew the now gathered, originally 7" long pieces of ribbon to the wrong side of the middle 5" piece, overlapping ⅛".

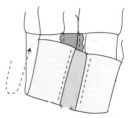

Fold inside out, right sides together and stitch or glue seams.

Turn right side out through one of the ends. Insert stuffing through one of the ends. Distribute stuffing so that it is evenly distributed, primarily in the two ends.

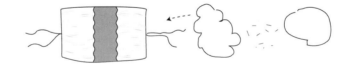

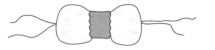

Pull on wires to gather, pouf, and close ends.

Twist wires, dip in glue, then stuff to the inside of the poufs. Glue the rosettes to cover holes at ends. Before gluing, place beaded, tiny silk ribbons for dangling effect.

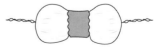

Time: 30 Minutes   **Skill Level: Advanced**   **Cost: $–$$**

MINIATURE SATIN ROSE FAVORS

Sweet little wrapped satin roses provide the inspiration for this favor grouping. The tiny buds can be used to enhance a placecard, a heart-shaped box, or top off a charming topiary.

Satin Rose Placecard

Ivory Pictureframe Placecard
Approximately 100–105 satin ribbon roses
Thick clear-drying scrapbook paste
Paintbrush or sponge applicator (optional)

Smooth paste over entire frame surface. Place roses into paste in a random pattern, covering the frame completely. Press rose bottoms firmly into the paste to make sure they adhere. Make sure to keep bottom edge line of roses straight so that the placecard can stand correctly.

Time: 10 minutes   **Skill Level: Beginner**   **Cost: $$**

Satin Rose Covered Box

2″ Diameter paper maché heart-shaped box
Acrylic paint in ivory
Sponge type brush applicator
100 mini satin ribbon roses
Thick clear-drying scrapbook paste

Paint box on the inside and out with the ivory paint. Let dry thoroughly. Put lid on box. Draw a faint line on the bottom of the box to indicate where the lid sits so that you won't glue the mini roses too high up on the box and keep the lid from seating properly. Remove lid. Apply paste in a nice thick coat on the lid tops and sides. Press roses into the paste in a random fashion, beginning with the sides and finishing off with the lid. Press and mold the roses into the paste with your hands to ensure a good "fit".

Apply paste to box around the sides (take care not to go above your pencil marks), down to the bottom edge of the box. Press roses on sides, being careful to cover completely. Let dry.

Time: 15 minutes   **Skill Level: Beginner**   **Cost: $$**

Satin Rosebud Topiary

1½″ Glass votive holder
Green florist foam
Green moss
6″ Green wooden floral pick or small wooden dowel
12″ Satin ivory satin ribbon, 1″ wide
Double-sided super sticky tape
2″ Styrofoam ball
Approximately 100 mini satin ribbon roses
Thick clear-drying scrapbook paste
2 Yards soft rose colored sheer organza ribbon, ¼″ wide
2 Yards soft green colored sheer organza ribbon, ¼″ wide
6–5 small straight pins
Hot glue

Shape a piece of green florist foam to fit into the glass votive. Before placing into votive, wrap the green moss around the outside of the foam, then push into the votive. You should not see any of the foam through the glass, only the moss. Hot glue more moss on to the top of the foam and moss in the votive to give it a full crowning effect.

Wrap stick with double-sided sticky tape. Place 1" wide satin ribbon at an angle and wrap the stick, overlapping the edges of the ribbon so that none of the stick shows through. Leave 1½" of the stick uncovered at the bottom for easier insertion into the florist foam later on.

Push top of stick into the 2" Styrofoam ball, going in about 1". Apply thick paste to entire Styrofoam ball. Push satin ribbon roses into the paste, covering the entire ball. Keep the roses close together to avoid having any Styrofoam show through. When the ball is completely covered, use your hand to "cup" the ball and really push the roses into the paste.

Cut three 12" strips of the rose ribbon and three 12" strips of the green ribbon. With each strip, make a 3 loop, 2 tail bow. To do this, leave a tail 4" long, make three loops of ribbon of approximately ½" and pinch between your fingers. This should leave you with another tail of about 4" long. Secure the 3 loop, 2 tail bow into place with straight pins. Apply to bottom of ball, alternating green and rose. Trim tails.

With remaining ribbon, cut 2" lengths. Form double loop and "push" into ball with point of scissors in a random pattern. Put a double loop cluster at the base of the stick, pushing into Styrofoam.

Time: 30 minutes   Skill Level: Intermediate   Cost: $$

A GARDEN OF BATH CRYSTALS

For a festive, garden-like touch, surprise your guests with brightly colored and heavenly scented bath crystals. Wrap each one with a beautiful satin ribbon and top off with a silk or paper flower in coordinating colors. Placing them in a tin gardening bucket or terra cotta flowerpot is the perfect finishing touch.

VALENTINE'S DAY

While Valentine's Day most likely won't be a theme for your shower, tea, or luncheon, we couldn't resist these fun Valentine gifts and favors. The Cookie Topiary makes a fun project, a thoughtful hostess gift, or a perfect little "just because" present. Hershey's Kisses Roses are one of the easiest favors to make and, besides Valentine's Day, work wonderfully well for weddings. If you are planning on using them for weddings, you might want to consider other colors of cellophane to coordinate with the colors you are using for your wedding. Candy is a Valentine's Day staple, whether in dishes, charming little shopping bags, or wrapped in delicate tulle and accented with a ribbon. An organza bag can be embellished with a tiny red ribbon holding a dangling gold heart charm, and even your placecards can be decorated with tiny conversation hearts, because really, every day is a good day to say 'I Love You'.

Conversation Heart Placecard

White Pictureframe Placecard
Approximately 45 conversation hearts
Hot glue

Use the hot glue and affix hearts to the frame. Place some flat, some at angles, some slightly tilted for a random, whimsical effect.

Time: 10 minutes   **Skill Level: Beginner**   **Cost: $$**

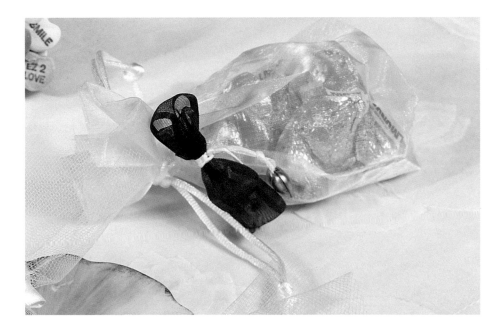

Valentine's Organza Bag

White organza bag, measuring 3˝ across and 5˝ long
8˝ Sheer red wired organza ribbon with satin edges, ⅝˝ wide
2 3˝ lengths white satin ribbon, ¹⁄₁₆˝ wide
1 gold heart charm with loop for hanging, ½˝ – ⅝˝ long
Hot glue

Take the red ribbon and fold the bottom 1½" under.

Make another fold 2½" from that. Form another fold 2" from the second and then fold the last in back under the other piece so it doesn't show.

Take the two pieces of ¹⁄₁₆" ribbon and, holding them together, knot at both ends, leaving about ¼" ribbon hanging past the knots. Then pinch the center of the folded red ribbon and use the ¹⁄₁₆" ribbon to tie and secure. Hot glue the ribbon cluster onto the organza bag just below the drawstring line.

Hot glue the charm to one of the knotted ends by slipping one of the ¼" "tails" into the loop and securing it all with a dab of hot glue.

Time: 10 minutes **Skill Level: Beginner** **Cost: $$**

Valentine Cookie Topiary

3½" x 3½" flower pot
Green florist foam
Green Spanish Moss
Hot glue
3 6" Wooden green floral picks
3 Decorated heart-shaped thick sugar cookies
2 Hershey's Kisses "Roses" made with floral picks instead of green cloth-covered wire (directions below)
18" Ivory satin ribbon, ¼" wide
Spray crackle medium
Gold acrylic paint
Linen acrylic paint
Sponge applicator
Hot glue

When Making Cookies:

When you take the sugar cookies out of the oven, while they are still on the hot cookie tray, immediately insert the floral pick into the cookie. Insert it at the point of the heart, about 1½" deep into the cookie. (This will be easier if you have used a flat "lipless" cookie sheet or have only placed the cookies in the center of the sheet.) Let cool. Decorate as desired.

To Decorate Pot:

Apply gold paint to flowerpot using sponge applicator. Let dry. Apply crackle medium to the area below the rim of the flowerpot. Following manufacturer's instructions, while still tacky, apply a thin coat of linen-colored acrylic paint using a smearing technique. As the paint dries, the crackle finish will emerge.

Put florist foam into decorated pot. Apply hot glue to the top and cover with Spanish moss, letting it fluff and drape a bit for a natural, random effect.

Insert the cookies on a stick into the foam at different depths for a varied effect. Then insert the two Hershey's Roses. Tie a ribbon around the foremost rose.

Time: 30 minutes   **Skill Level: Beginner**   **Cost: $$**

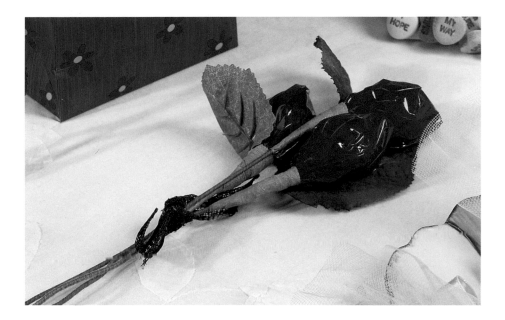

Hershey's Kisses Roses

2 Hershey's Kisses
Red cellophane, 4″ x 4″
Thick green tape covered wire OR
6″ Green florist picks
2″ Leaf with a ½″ stem
Spool of green floral tape

Place the kisses base to base. Holding the red cellophane in your hand, push the tip of one of the kisses into the center of the cellophane. Gather the cellophane up and around both kisses. Secure cellophane ends by taking the florist tape and wrapping around three times. Make sure to pull the tape nice and tight. Insert stick into the gathered cellophane base, twist the tape two more times. Lay the stem of the leaf up against the wire or floral pick, wrap the tape around to capture the stem and keep on wrapping all the way down the pick or wire, keeping the tape tight and at an angle. Snip tape when you reach the end and pinch it to stick to wire.

Time: 3 minutes　　　　　**Skill Level: Beginner**　　　　　**Cost: $**

A GARDEN PARTY

An outdoor garden party is one of the most casual, relaxed surroundings in which to throw a shower or luncheon. The out of doors provides an ideal setting for your party, with the natural greenery and flowers acting as the perfect backdrop.

Whenever you entertain out of doors, it takes a bit of extra planning to make things just perfect. Attention to the little details, aesthetic as well as logistical, can make all the difference in how smoothly the occasion goes.

Our Garden Party Collection wonderfully captures the flavor of the outdoors, from the whimsical butterfly topiary, to the charming dragonfly on the paper sculpture placecard. We show another version of our Pretty Corner Sachet Pocket, this one in warm tones and accented with a golden bumble bee charm. Earth tones are picked up in the votive holder, the decoupage base of the topiary, as well as the plates and linens. No time to make anything? That won't be a problem. Guests will delight in decorated soaps, charming country-themed "stick-it" type notes, or enchanting boxes filled with dried lavender.

Butterfly Topiary

3″ Terra cotta flower pot
Green florist foam
Green moss
3 Sheets natural earth toned rice or textured papers, 8″ x 11″ each
1 Metal butterfly on 6″ stick with "rusted" finish
2 12″ Lengths of rusted finish metal strips, ⅛″ wide
Hot glue
Decoupage glue
Sponge tip paint brush

Rip pieces of earth-toned textured papers into randomly shaped pieces of approximately 2" x 2" in size. Apply decoupage glue to the back of each piece of paper and lay on pot. Mix the different papers to give a natural, patchwork effect. Cover the pot entirely. When completely covered, apply a coat of decoupage glue over the entire pot.

NOTE: Make sure to carry your paper strips up and over the top to the inside "lip" of the pot.

Insert florist foam into the pot.

Apply hot glue to top of foam and press green moss into place. Let some of the moss fall over the edge of the pot for a natural, hanging effect.

Push butterfly decoration into the center of foam, pushing the stick 1½" into the foam.

Using craft scissors, cut the ⅛" strips of rusty-finished metal and cluster together. Push them into the pot and bend slightly to create the same effect as a blade of grass.

Time: 30 minutes   **Skill Level: Beginner**   **Cost: $$**

Pretty Corner Sachet Pockets

10″ Square fabric
10″ Square inexpensive sheer fabric
¾ Cup dried flower potpourri
1 Metal bumblebee charm
20″ Ivory organza ribbon, 1½″ wide
20″ Gold organza ribbon, ⅝″ wide
Hot glue

Cut 10" square of fabric.

Place on table with wrong side up.

Fold all edges over ¼", press, then use hot glue to glue them in place.

Cut 10" piece of inexpensive, sheer fabric.

Lay flat on table, wrong side up.

Fill with ¾ cup of pretty dried flower potpourri.

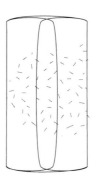

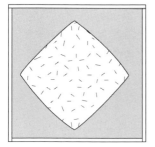

Fold both sides to middle, overlapping about 1 – 2".

Repeat with top and bottom to form a wrapped packet of about 3 – 3½".

Place sheer packet fold-side down in the center of the finished edge fabric from step one. Finished edge fabric should be wrong side up, and packet should sit on the wrong side.

Place a dab of hot glue smaller than a dime onto the center of the sheer packet.

Bring four corners of outside fabric into the middle.

Press each of the four corners into the hot glue.

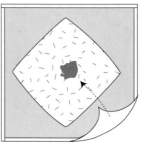

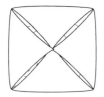

To Decorate Center:

Using both ribbons at once, tie a bow. Knot ends. Hot glue bow to center of packet. Hot glue bumblebee charm in center of bow.

Time: 10–12 min   **Skill Level: Intermediate**   **Cost: $–$$**

Dragonfly Placecard

Placecard in ivory, 3½″ x 4″, that folds to 3½″ x 2″ (purchased)
"Crushed" and wrinkled gold paper, 1⅞″ x 3⅛″
Green leaf tissue paper, ⅞″ x 1⅜″
Orange natural leaf paper, 2¹⁄₁₆″ x ¾″
Ivory card stock, 1⅝″ x ¾″
Brass decorative dragonfly charm
Clear-drying scrapbook paste
Krazy or Super Glue

Apply scrapbook paste to the "crushed" and wrinkled gold paper and adhere it to the ivory notecard, making sure to center it. In the order listed above, which is working largest to smallest, apply all the different pieces of paper. (See photo for placement or refer to page 139.)

Use Super Glue to affix dragonfly charm to front of placecard at an angle, to the right of center. Use only a small dab as it will leave a "watermark" stain on the tissue if you use too much. Hold dragonfly in place until glue begins to dry.

Time: 7 minutes   Skill Level: Beginner   Cost: $$

Natural Paper Decoupaged Votive Holder

Glass votive cup with flared lip, 2″ high
Natural earth-toned rice or textured papers, torn into small, irregular
  shaped pieces
Decoupage glue
Sponge tip applicator
Raffia strips in natural and green, 9″ each
Votive candle
Hot glue

Tear enough strips of paper to entirely cover the glass votive holder.
Apply decoupage glue to the backs of the paper strips using the applicator.
Apply to the votive holder one at a time using a random pattern. Make
sure to completely cover the glass. When completely covered, apply a coat
of decoupage glue over the entire pot. Let dry.

Twist the two strands of raffia together and wrap them around the
votive, knotting once in front, then bringing to the back and knotting
again. Use a dab of hot glue to anchor.

Time: 10 minutes   **Skill Level: Beginner**   **Cost: $**

FEMININE APPEAL

The delicate warm pink of hydrangea blossoms capture the essence of this favors grouping. Pick up the dainty colors with a beautifully woven ribbon box, or a tea light decorated with colorful beads. (Warning: This ribbon box is very time consuming, but lovely. You will most likely *not* want to make a large number of these!) A silken tassel accents the floral placecard. Pick an element that works for your skill level and budget, then have fun enchanting your guests.

Floral Tassel Placecard

Pictureframe Placecard
Wrapping paper, 3½″ x 5″
Ivory tassel, 2″ long
Bead mixture (here we used tiny opalescent pink beads, micro gold
  beads, and irregular, "rock" shaped pink and coral beads)
Thick clear-drying craft paste
Decoupage glue
Paintbrush or sponge applicator (optional)
Hot glue

Pop the back off of placecard. Cut wrapping paper into general shape of placecard and, using decoupage glue, "wallpaper" the frame with the wrapping paper, being careful to smooth inside oval edges. Apply dab of scrapbook paste about the size of a dime to upper left corner of frame. Press tassel into the paste. Sprinkle beads into the paste and press to secure. Place a smaller dab of the scrapbook paste in the bottom right hand corner of the frame. Press beads into paste. Glue back of frame back into place with hot glue. Make sure to leave open across bottom so you can slide the name card into place.

Time: 6 minutes   Skill Level: Beginner   Cost: $$

Hydrangea Cone Topiary

Foam cone shaped base measuring 2″ wide
  at the base and 5″ high (you may need
  to buy a larger cone and trim the top off
  to size)

3″ x 3½″ Terra cotta flowerpot

Ivory "Stone Effect" spray paint

Gray Spanish moss

Green florist foam

6″ Green wooden floral stick or dowel

12″ Ivory satin ribbon, 1 wide

16″ Floral embroidered ribbon (soft pink
  color), ⅝″ wide

11″ Soft, light green grosgrain ribbon, ½″
  wide

1 Stem of blush-colored hydrangea,
  approximately 20 heads

1 Stem ivory colored foam faux wheat
  cluster, approx. 20″

1 Stem blush/pink small orchid,
  approximately 18 heads

Double-sided sticky tape

Hot glue

Thick clear-drying scrapbook paste

Spray flower pot with the stone effect paint, covering with three coats, inside and out. Let dry completely between coats.

Fill pot with florist foam.

Cover top of florist foam with hot glue and cover with the gray Spanish moss. Let some spill over for a natural, cascading effect.

Cover the floral stick or dowel with the double-sided sticky tape. Place the 1" wide ivory satin ribbon at the top of the dowel, about 1½" down from the top edge. Going at an angle, wrap around stick. Make sure to overlap edges so that the stick is completely covered. End the ribbon about 2½" to 3" above the bottom edge of the stick.

Apply thick, clear-drying scrapbook paste to cone and cover with thin layer of gray moss. Make sure to cover bottom of cone.

Press and shape moss with hands.

The flowers are applied to the cone in a spiral direction. Start with the wheat first, cutting long pieces from the stem and laying it on the cone, working from the bottom to the top. Leave a ¾" space between spiral "rows." Apply the hot glue in strips just big enough to adhere the wheat strip you're working with or it will dry before you can get to it.

Next, working from the bottom of the cone, glue heads of the orchids, continuing to spiral up. Follow with a row of hydrangea heads, also working bottom to top and spiraling. The goal is to completely cover the cone with the spiraling rows of flowers.

Insert ribbon-covered stick into cone about 2" deep and insert the other end into the base, about 3½" deep. Finished topiary should stand about 10½" high.

Using the embroidered ⅝" ribbon, form a "bow" by making three 1" loops of ribbon then pinching. This should leave two tails of 5" each. Use a small dab of hot glue in the middle to hold loops in place.

Repeat the above using the soft green ½" wide grosgrain ribbon and forming three loops of ¾" in the middle, leaving two 4" tails. Use a dab of hot glue in middle to hold.

Place a small puddle of hot glue (about the size of a nickel) in the Spanish moss at the base of the ribbon-covered stick. Push the embroidered bow into hot glue, pushing the bow all the way down to the foam. Put dab of glue on the back of pinch loops on the green bow and push down on top of and into the embroidered bow.

Time: 30 minutes   Skill Level: Intermediate   Cost:$$$

Woven Ribbon Box

Paper maché box with lid, 2¼″ x 2½″
Iron on double-sided fusible interfacing 6″ x 6″
Ivory brocade fabric, 8″ x 8″
2 Pieces ivory satin fabric, 1 — 8″ x 8″, 1 — 3¼″ x 3¼″
10″ Satin floral multi-colored ribbon trim, ¹⁄₁₆″ wide, for outside of lid
6½″ Satin floral multi-colored ribbon trim, for inside bow
11″ Length soft green grosgrain ribbon, ½″ wide

Ribbons for Weaving:
Soft green grosgrain, ½″ wide — 4 strips 5½″ long, total = 22″
Ivory Satin, ¼″ wide — 4 strips 5½″ long, total = 22″
Pink Satin, ¼″ wide — 4 strips 5½″ long, total = 22″
Embroidered satin, ⅝″ wide, 2 strips 5½″ long, total = 11″

Soft board for pinning and weaving ribbons
(Use 8″ x 11″ piece of cardboard. Cover with wash cloth and tape to
  board. This leaves you a nice surface to pin into.)
Straight pins
Hot glue
Fabric glue

Cover inside of lid by folding raw edges under ¼" on 3¼" x 3¼" piece of ivory satin and press. Using fabric glue, glue fabric into lid being careful not to let corners get too thick. Let dry.

To cover outside bottom of box with brocade fabric, set the box down in the middle of the WRONG side of the brocade (the RIGHT side of the brocade will be facing the table). "Wrap" the brocade up around the box as you would a present, coming up and inside the box about 1". Make sure to press the folds very flat. Glue with fabric glue. NOTE: You really need to flatten the corners so they don't bunch too much or the lid will not sit on the box properly. Test fit the lid onto the box before the glue on the corners of the bottom dries.

Fold the raw edges under a ¼" on the 8" x 8" ivory satin fabric. With edges folded down, hot glue the fabric into the box, beginning about ¼" to ½" down from the top lip of the bottom of the box. As you glue, make sure and let the fabric drape and puff up inside of box for a less severe effect.

Using a 6½" piece of multi-colored satin trim, tie a bow and glue it into inside corner of box using the hot glue.

To Weave Top of Lid:

Start by peeling off plastic coating from one side of fusible interfacing. Place in center of soft board. Lay the first piece of ⅝" embroidered ribbon in the center of the interfacing. To the right of that ribbon, lay a piece of pink ribbon, then soft green grosgrain ribbon, then ivory. To the left of the center ribbon, lay the ivory, soft green grosgrain, then pink ribbons down in that order. Using the pins, secure both sides of the ribbon to the soft board so that they are held in place nice and tight.

Beginning in the center again, take a piece of ⅝" embroidered ribbon and begin weaving it in and out of the secured ribbons. Using the same order as above, repeat the process with the other six ribbons, keeping the ribbons nice and tight as you weave. Pin in place.

Press ribbon to interfacing following the manufacturer's instructions. Lift from soft board and peel off underside plastic coating from interfacing and iron/fuse to top of box. Make sure to center pattern, fold over edges, and press. Cut around lid so all ribbons are about ⅛" short of top of lid.

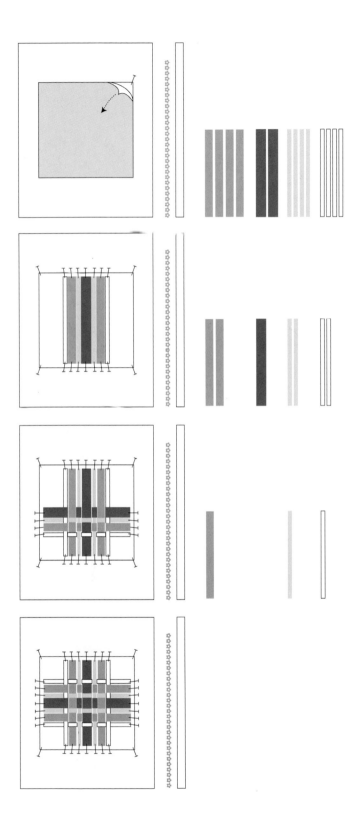

Fabric glue the green ½" ribbon around the bottom edge of the lid to cover up all cut edges of ribbon. Hot glue decorative "loop" ribbon trim.

Tim: 45 minutes   **Skill Level: Advanced**   **Cost: $$**

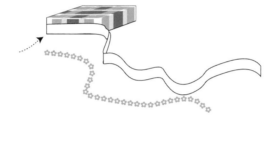

Beaded Tea Light

Plastic tea light, ¾″ high x 1½″ diameter
Double-sided super sticky craft tape
Bead mix
Tea light

Put strip of tape around outside rim of tea light. Roll in beads, pressing to make sure they adhere. Add tea light.

Time: 2 minutes　　　　　**Skill Level: Beginner**　　　　　**Cost $**

NECESSARY INDULGENCES

Few women can resist the lure of luxurious bath products and your guests will be no exception, especially when they see how charmingly you've decorated them. Small boxes of indulgent bath oil beads are available in a variety of colors and fragrances. They have the added bonus of needing only a bit of pretty ribbon for decoration, and perhaps a feather or two. Bars of creamy fragrant soap also lend themselves especially well

to ribbon accents, but don't stop there. Try silver cording with a feather accent, or perhaps add a silk or paper flower for a festive look. Soap can also be wrapped or gathered in pretty handkerchiefs, which make the favor actually two gifts in one. For a striking presentation, wrap the bars of soap in pretty rice paper or heavily textured corrugated paper. Enhance with a woven ribbon or a bit of raffia and a small leaf or twig.

LAVENDER

Capture the feel of a fresh spring day with these vibrant favors. The lavender on the topiary picks up the lilac color found in the dainty trim accenting the doily sachet. Perfect for a shower, luncheon, or tea, or anytime you're in the mood for a touch of spring.

Triangle Style Doily Sachet

1 9″ Square fabric doily (purchased at fabric or craft stores)
18″ Decorative trim
9″ ⅛″ Wide ribbon in green
18″ ⅛″ Wide ribbon in lilac (cut into two 9″ pieces)
Miniature Calla lillies (can be any flower of your choice)
¾ Cup dacron stuffing (can be lightly scented with potpourri oil —
    see page 16)

Fold square doily into triangle.

Apply hot glue along open edges of triangle leaving a 1½″ wide opening for stuffing

TIP: It is easier and looks smoother if you leave the opening along one of the straight edges of the triangle as opposed to trying to leave the opening at a corner.

After glue dries, insert stuffing into triangle using small blunt object (like the eraser edge of a pencil or a small dowel) to fill stuffing into triangle points.

Glue opening shut, making sure not to catch any stuffing in the seam.

Hot glue decorative trim along the joint where the lace meets the body of the doily fabric.

TIP: Do not begin at a corner. It is easier to hide the joining of the two ends of decorative trim if they meet along a straight edge as opposed to a corner.

Twist the wire stems of the flower cluster together. Put a dab of hot glue ⅛″ below the base of the flowers. Trim off all but ⅛″ of the wire stems.

Put dab of hot glue on back of flower cluster, then press onto pillow.

Holding all three strands of 9″ long ribbon, tie a bow. Place a dab of hot glue on the back of bow. Press into place on pillow, making sure to cover up wire stems. Trim ribbon stems at an angle.

Time: 10-15 minutes per sachet

Skill Level: Beginner

Cost: $

Lavender Topiary

Terra cotta flowerpot, 2½"

Green florist foam

Green moss

6" Wooden floral pick

2" Styrofoam ball

½ Cup dried lavender

Thick clear-drying scrapbook paste

Acrylic paint in lavender

Acrylic paint in dark lavender

24" Lavender satin ribbon, ⅛" wide

12" Lavender and white striped grosgrain
  ribbon, ⅛" wide

Sponge applicator

Hot glue

Paint pot and dowel with lavender paint. Let dry. Hightlight top edge of pot with dark lavender paint, dabbing on with a sponge brush.

Fill pot with foam. Cover top with hot glue and apply green moss. Pile up the moss so it "crowns" the pot.

Push stick into Styrofoam ball about 1". With finger, apply craft paste to entire surface of Styrofoam ball. Place ½ cup dried lavender on paper plate and roll paste-covered ball on the plate, covering with lavender. Push lavender into place on the paste with your hand.

Place stick with ball into center of foam in pot. Top of ball should be about 7" from bottom of pot.

Cut 24" lavender satin ribbon in half and gather all three ribbons. Tie into bow at the top of the stick. Use a dab of hot glue to hold in place. Trim ribbon ends and tie knots.

Time: 30 minutes   **Skill Level: Beginner**   **Cost: $$**

VARYING ELEMENTS

Here we show how the merest change in an element or two can give the favor a whole new look and feel. In this topiary, we've once again used hydrangea blossoms, but mixed them with grape vine clusters and placed them all in a more ornate urn. The whole topiary takes on a more stately, elegant feel.

We've also provided a different look for our Hankie Envelope Style Sachet. Here we've used a crisp white handkerchief with white thread embroidery. We've accented it all with a dainty trim of pink flowers and green "leaves" for a fresh new look.

Hankie "Envelope" Style Sachet

1 Square hankie (Can be found at yard sales, thrift shops, antique stores, or swap meets)

¾ Cup potpourri or dacron stuffing

16″ small rose ribbon trim

Small white button, ¼″ wide

Hot glue

Fold square hankie in half to form a triangle.

Bring left corner into center, keeping bottom edge aligned.

Bring left point 1" past center of triangle.

Fold over the right edge in the same way, bringing the right point all the way to the left fold. Do not overlap past the edge of the hankie.

Apply thin strip of hot glue ⅛" up from the bottom edge. Press firmly and make sure no glue oozes out. Apply another strip of hot glue along second bottom edge, and press top glued fold into that glue, in effect gluing all three folded edges together.

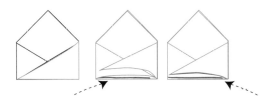

Peel apart the two layers of hankie on the top point of the "envelope." Place potpourri between the two layers, and shake down to fill so that it doesn't spill back out of the top.

Fold top over like envelope, gluing closed along V. Press into place.

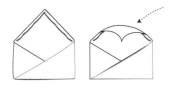

Hot glue rose trim into place along the V of the envelope. Finish off in the center with a small bow made of the trim. Top with button.

Time: 10 minutes   **Skill level: Beginner**   **Cost: $–$$**
(depending on cost of hankie)

Hydrangea and Grape Vine Cluster Topiary

3″ x 3½″ Decorative clay or resin flowerpot

Florist foam

Green moss

3″ Styrofoam ball

1 Stem, approximately 36″ of soft blush silk hydrangea

1 Stem, artificial raspberry ball cluster, cut into approximately
   20 small clusters

3 Grape vine twigs approximately 6″ long

Floral wire

Thick clear-drying scrapbook paste

Hot glue

Fill pot with foam. Cover top with hot glue and press green moss into place, allowing moss to fall over edge a bit for a tumbling effect.

Twist grape vine twigs together to create a natural "trunk" for the ball to sit on. Secure twigs at the top and bottom with floral wire.

Cover 3" ball with thick craft paste and apply a thin layer of moss with hands. Cupping your hand, "press" moss into place to completely cover the ball.

Push twig trunk into the foam ball about 1½" deep. Make sure this is secure.

Snip flower heads off of stem and using a hot glue gun secure flowers to ball in a random flowing pattern. Allow space between flower cluster for a natural effect. Trail some of the blossoms down the ball onto the twig trunk.

Snip small cluster of raspberry balls and glue onto flowers.

(NOTE: This is the strongest color element so don't be too heavy with these.)

Glue a few flower heads and clusters into the pot at the base of the twig trunk.

Remember, less is best in order to give the most natural garden effect.

Time: 30 minutes   **Skill Level: Advanced**   **Cost: $$$**

Bird in Grape Vine Wreath Topiary

3½" x 3½" Decorative pot in moss gray/green
30" Wired grapevine in plum color
Painted bird in mushroom color, approximately 1½" long
Gray Spanish moss
Green florist foam
Hot glue
3 Sturdy grapevine "twigs" in realistic brown color, 8" long
6 Short pieces of wire
18" Moss-colored organza ribbon, ⅝" wide
42" Soft blush-colored organza ribbon, ¼" wide

Fill pot with florist foam. Cover florist foam with hot glue and apply gray Spanish moss. Pile the moss on so that it "crowns" above top of pot around where the stem will be. Allow moss to tumble out of the pot slightly for a natural cascading effect.

Twist the three 8" grape vine twigs together to form the trunk of the topiary. Hold twist together at top and bottom with short wire pieces.

Take the 30" length of plum-colored grapevine and, starting about 2" up from the bottom of the topiary "trunk", wrap the plum grapevine around the trunk. When you reach the end of the trunk, twist the grapevine around itself two times to form a circle of about 3½" in diameter. The grapevine has wire in the center of it and should hold its shape quite nicely. Continue twisting the grapevine back down the trunk. Secure the circle to the trunk using the last two pieces of wire.

Take a 20" piece of gray moss and roll it into a 20" long tube with a diameter resembling that of a breadstick. Wind this "tube" around the trunk and wreath in order to hide the wire. Fluff out any leaves that have been caught under the moss.

Hot glue the bird into a nest of leaves and moss in the wreath at about a 7 o'clock position.

Take the moss-colored organza ⅝" ribbon and form a bow, with two tails of 5½" and three loops 1" each. Secure with wire.

Cut the blush-colored organza ribbon into three equal lengths. Fold in half and wire to the green bow, 1" down from the fold. This will result in three loops (above the wire) and six tails (falling below the wire).

Glue bow to topiary at bottom right side of circle. Trim ends.

Time: 30 minutes   **Skill Level: Advanced**   **Cost: $$–$$$**

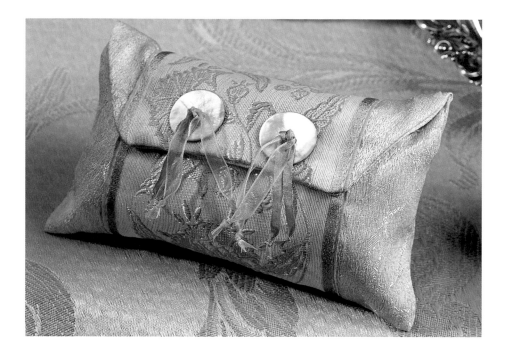

Brocade Envelope Style Sachet

2 Pieces brocade patterned antique satin, 6″ x 9″ each

9″ Piece of embroidered organza ribbon, 3½″ wide

2 Abalone buttons, ⅜″ diameter

12″ Light purple silk ribbon, ⅛″ wide

12″ Blush organza ribbon, ⅛″ wide

Embroidery needle with eye big enough to thread ribbon (Also needs to be small enough to fit through the holes in the button.)

Hot glue

Scented dacron stuffing (page 16)

Stitch the 3½" wide ribbon to the RIGHT side of one of the 6" x 9" rectangles, making sure to center it evenly. Run the seam lengthwise, as close to the edge of the ribbon as possible.

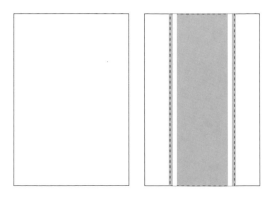

Place the two 6" x 9" rectangles with RIGHT sides together. Cut the envelope shape out of the top of the fabric. The width of the flap should be 4" at the top and come down at an angle until it hits the side at 2½" down.

Stitch around entire rectangle, leaving 1" open on side for turning right side out. Use ¼" seam allowances

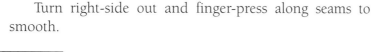

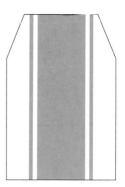

Turn right-side out and finger-press along seams to smooth.

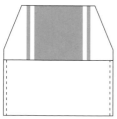

Fold bottom 3" of rectangle. With fold facing you, stitch folded flap in place at sides using a ¼" seam allowance.

Turn right side out. This should look like an envelope.
Fill with stuffing.

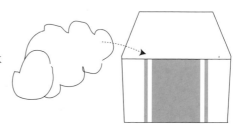

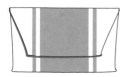

Hot glue closed.
Cut both 12" lengths of ribbon in half. Using embroidery needle, thread ribbon through holes in the button. Knot in place, and knot the ends.

Glue ribbon-threaded abalone buttons right above flap.

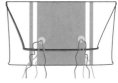

Time: 20 minutes   **Skill Level: Intermediate**   **Cost: $$–$$$**

Square Votive Candle

Square votive candle in sage green
12–14″ Silk ribbon, ½″ wide
Sealing wax
Seal
Hot glue

Wrap ribbon around votive. Affix with hot glue. Make wax seal on a separate sheet of wax paper and apply to ribbon with hot glue.

Time: 2 minutes   **Skill Level: Beginner**   **Cost: $**

Purchased Favors — Showers, Teas, and Luncheons

Pretty in Pink Tea — Page 54
    Perfume Bottles $$–$$$
    Decorated Soap $$$
    Decorated Box filled with lavender $$$–$$$$

Peachy Bridesmaid's Luncheon — Page 66
    Small Painted Box $$
    Frosted Perfume Bottles $$–$$$$
    Fizzy Bath Balls $$
    Martini Style glass dish $$
    Tin Bucket $

Garden of Bath Crystals — Page 82 $$

Garden Party — Page 88
    Stick On Notes $$
    Decorated boxes filled with lavender $$$–$$$$
    Decorated Soap $$$

Necessary Indulgences — Page 106
    Bath Oil Beads $$–$$$
    Aromatherapy Kit $$$
    Soaps $–$$$

Varying Elements — Page 118
    Ribbon Wrapped Frosted Votive $$
    Ribbon Wrapped Pillar $
    Ornate Sachet $$$$$

DINNER PARTY
FAVORS

UCH OF OUR ENTERTAINING takes place around the dining table. Whether small, intimate gatherings of a few friends and family, or large, elaborate productions, dinner parties tend to be the focal point of our entertaining lives. The age-old custom of gathering around a table to break bread together goes far back into our historic pasts where alliances were forged, treaties sealed, and betrothals agreed upon. Oftentimes we entertain for professional reasons, to come together with our business associates for a more casual, personal gathering, but mostly we use dinner parties as a primary form of social connection, a perfect way to spend time with our friends and acquaintances in a relaxed and gracious atmosphere.

Even for the most casual of gatherings, it takes no more than a small touch here and there to make the evening truly special and out of the ordinary. A small elegantly decorated soap or sachet showcased among your finest china and sparkling crystal can make quite a statement. Consider the warm, intimate glow of small candles and votives liberally sprinkled with beads in wonderful rich, jewel tones. Or perhaps you'd prefer to gild them with gold leaf. Once again, you needn't be limited to items you can make. The possibilities for favors for these types of occasions are almost endless.

Keep in mind, the dining table can be anywhere you choose. Pool parties, barbecues, dining "al fresco," and beach-themed gatherings all present wonderful opportunities for coming together in the spirit of friendship.

Beaded and Gilded Flowerpot Votive Holder

2″ Terra cotta flower pot
Gold leafing
Matte drying decoupage glue
Bead mixture
2 Sponge applicators
Gold acrylic paint
Thick clear-drying scrapbook paste
Tweezers

Completely cover the flowerpot with decoupage glue. Pick up a piece of leafing and using the second, clean sponge tip applicator, pat it in place and crinkle it slightly. (NOTE: The leafing will dull slightly when it touches the wet glue, but when it dries it will regain its original shine.) Take the leafing up to the lip of the pot. (Use gold acrylic paint to paint the inside of the pot—gold leafing is too expensive to use where it won't show.) When the pot is completely dry, cover with a thin layer of decoupage glue to seal in the leafing. Let dry. Apply thick coat of paste to rim of flowerpot. Sprinkle the bead mixture into the paste, using your fingers, and press down to make the beads adhere firmly.

Time: 15 minutes   **Skill Level: Beginner**   **Cost:$$**

Vellum Wrapped Votive

Glass votive cup, 2″ in diameter and 2½″ high
Vellum, 2½″ wide by 7¼″ long, cut straight or with deckled edge
22″ gold cord
1 votive candle
Super sticky double-sided craft tape

Place strip of super sticky double-sided tape lengthwise in back of votive. Cover ½ of the strip of tape with the beginning edge of the vellum. Wrap vellum around glass votive, making sure to finish with edge being pressed into the remaining piece of tape. Wrap the gold cording around the votive twice, beginning and ending in the front. Tie a knot, then knot both ends to finish off cording and keep from fraying. Place candle in cup.

Time: 3 minutes   Skill Level: Beginner   Cost: $$

Square Bead Covered Votive Candle

Square votive candle, 2″
**Bead mixture (We used dark blue, gold, dark green, and purple in
  small round and "rice" shaped beads.)**
Thick clear-drying scrapbook paste
Decoupage glue (for sealing)
Sponge tip applicator

Cover all four sides of the candle with the paste. Sprinkle the beads
into the paste, using your fingers to press firmly so that the beads adhere
securely. Very gently, use the decoupage glue to seal.

Time: 6 minutes   Skill Level: Beginner   Cost: $

Square Gold Leafed Votive Candle

Square votive candle, 2″
Matte drying decoupage glue
Gold leafing, 15–16 nickel size pieces
Sponge tip applicator
Tweezers

Apply decoupage glue to the four sides of the candle as well as the top.
Using the tweezers, if necessary, apply the leafing to the candle, then use
the sponge tip applicator to pat down and crinkle. When finished, apply
a thin coat of decoupage glue over the entire candle to seal.

Time: 3 minutes   Skill Level: Beginner   Cost: $

Split Corner Pocket Sachet

10″ Square fabric
10″ Square inexpensive sheer fabric
¾ Cup dried flower potpourri
12″ Colored silk ribbon
1 Tablespoon colored beads
Hot glue

Cut 10″ square of fabric.
Place on table with wrong side up.

Fold all edges over ¼″, press, then use hot glue to glue them in place.

Cut 10" piece of inexpensive, sheer fabric.
Lay flat on table, wrong side up.
Fill with ¾ cup of pretty dried flower potpourri.

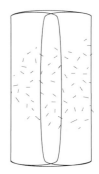

Fold both sides to middle, overlapping about 1" – 2".
Repeat with top and bottom to form a wrapped packet of about 3" – 3½". Hot glue packet closed.

Place sheer packet fold-side down in the center of the finished edge fabric from step one. Finished edge fabric should be wrong side up, and packet should sit on the wrong side.

Place a dab of hot glue smaller than a dime onto the center of the sheer packet. Bring four corners of outside fabric into the middle.

Press each of the four corners into the hot glue. Fabric should sink down into center glue spot.

Tie silk ribbon into a bow. Hot glue to center of sachet. Place small dab of hot glue on the top of bow knot. Sprinkle beads with glue.

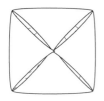

Apply a tiny bit of glue to each corner, then dip the corner into the beads. Repeat with all four corners.

Time: 10–12 minutes   Skill Level: Intermediate   Cost: $–$$

Bead Trim Wrapped Votive Holder

Glass votive cup with flared lip, 2″ high
7″ Dark blue beaded lace trim
Thick clear-drying scrapbook paste
Votive candle

Make sure votive cup is clean before starting. Apply paste to back side of the beaded lace. Press into place along middle of votive. While paste is still wet, use a damp paper towel to clean up any paste that has "leaked" out from under the lace.

Time: 2 minutes   Skill Level: Beginner   Cost: $$

Wrapped Beaded Wire Votive Holder

Glass votive holder, 2½″
36″ Thin gold craft wire
¼ Cup mixed beads in blues and greens
Toothpick
Needlenose pliers
Votive candle
Hot glue

String beads onto wire a few at a time. Crimp by wrapping beaded wire around a toothpick for a crinkled, artistic effect. When wire is finished, wrap the beaded wire around votive holder four times, beginning and ending in the front. Twist to secure. Crimp ends with needlenose pliers.

Time: 15 minutes   Skill Level: Intermediate   Cost: $$

Gold Cord Draped Placecard

Ivory Pictureframe Placecard
36″ Gold cording
Hot glue

Cut cording into two 16" strips and one 4" strip. Laying the two 16" strips together, tie a bow. Knot all four ends. Put a dab of hot glue on the upper left hand corner of the Pictureframe Placecard. Settle the knot of the bow into the dab of glue. Drape ends up and around the top of the frame, placing a dab of glue to hold in place, then another drop of glue where the one cord crosses over the other. Do the same with the ends of the bow that trail down the lefthand side of the frame.

Loop the 4" piece of cord into a double loop. On the bottom right hand corner, place loops. Turn frame over and hot glue the loops into place on the back side.

Time: 2 minutes   **Skill Level: Beginner**   **Cost: $**

Gold and Silver Leafed Votive Bowl

Bowl-shaped glass votive holder, 2″
Matte drying decoupage glue
Gold and silver leafing
Sponge tip applicator
Tweezers
Votive candle

Apply decoupage glue to the votive holder. Using the tweezers, if necessary, apply the leafing to the glass, then use the sponge tip applicator to pat down and crinkle. When finished, apply a thin coat of decoupage glue over the entire votive to seal.

Time: 7 minutes   **Skill Level: Beginner**   **Cost: $$**

Dangling Bead Trim Tea Light

Glass tea light holder, 1¾" x 1" high
6½" Beaded trim
Super or Krazy Glue
Tea light

As you cut the bead trim to size, watch to make sure the beads don't begin to unravel off the thread. If they do, use a drop of glue to seal edges. Apply glue to the entire strip of beading then press to tea light rim. Hold in place until it begins to seal.

Time: 3 minutes   **Skill Level: Beginner**   **Cost: $$**

Square Votive Candle with Bead Accent

Square votive candle, 2"
Bead mixture (We used dark blue, gold, dark green, and purple in small round and "rice" shaped beads.)
Thick clear-drying scrapbook paste
Decoupage glue (for sealing)
Sponge tip applicator

Apply paste in the design pattern you desire. Sprinkle the beads into the paste, using your fingers to press firmly so that the beads adhere securely. Very gently, use the decoupage glue to seal.

Time: 4 minutes   **Skill Level: Beginner**   **Cost: $**

Dragonfly Collage Placecard

Purchased placecard in ivory, 3½″ x 4″ that folds to 3½″ x 2″
"Crushed" and wrinkled gold paper, 1⅞″ x 3⅛″
Green leaf tissue paper, ⅞″ x 1⅜″
Orange natural leaf paper, 2¹⁄₁₆″ x ¾″
Ivory card stock, 1⅝″ x ¾″
Brass decorative dragonfly charm
Clear-drying scrapbook paste
Krazy or Super Glue

Apply scrapbook paste to the "crushed" and wrinkled gold paper and adhere it to the ivory notecard, making sure to center it. In the order listed above, which is working largest to smallest, apply all the different pieces of paper. (See diagram on next page.)

Use Super Glue to affix dragonfly charm to front of placecard at an angle, to the right of center. Use only a small dab as it will leave a "watermark" stain on the tissue if you use to much. Hold dragonfly in place until glue begins to dry.

Time: 8 minutes   Skill Level: Beginner   Cost: $

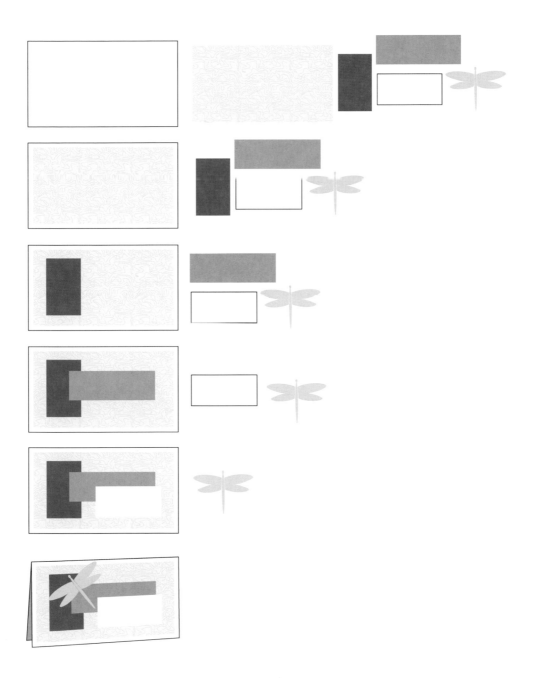

A TRADITIONAL SIT DOWN DINNER

There is a great deal of pleasure in taking out our finest china and silver in anticipation of a traditional sit down dinner. Nothing compares with the satisfaction of bringing together a group of your favorite people and treating them to your best hostessing skills. The time and care that go into planning a menu and preparing your carefully selected recipes is considerable. Luckily, selecting an appropriate favor doesn't have to be.

Beautiful collage style placecards can be made in under five minutes each, especially if you lay out all the materials ahead of time and proceed in an assembly line fashion. The beaded organza bag shown is deceptively simple to make, as is the wire mesh votive. Don't automatically assume that you need lots of time to put the favors together. Amidst the pressure of hosting an upcoming event, a profound sense of relaxation can be had by turning on some beautiful, soothing music and letting your hands be creative.

Bead Trimmed Organza Bag

Ivory organza bag measuring 3″ across and 5″ long with a flat bottom
2 6″ Pieces of ivory satin ribbon, ¼″ wide
2½″ Strip of dangling beads attached to ⅜″ ribbon
Hot glue

When you cut the bead trim, be careful the beads don't unravel off the threads you snipped. Seal the snipped threads with a spot of hot glue.

Take the flat bottom of the organza bag and fold it in half. Press. Open the fold. Apply hot glue to the wrong side of the beaded strip and lay it down on the back side of the fold. Apply another thin strip of hot glue to the top side of the bead trim, then press the front fold of the bottom onto that glue, so that you have, in effect, sealed the trim in the fold.

Take the two pieces of ivory ribbon and, holding them one on top of the other, tie into a bow. Hot glue onto the bag right below the drawstring. Hot glue one of the bead dangles into place on the front of the bow, tucking the thread it hangs on up into the knot of the bow to cover.

Time: 6 minutes   **Skill Level: Beginner**   **Cost: $$**

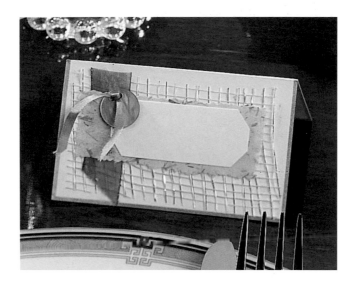

Wire Mesh and Abalone Button Collage Placecard

1 Silver-edged fold-over tent style placecard 3½″ x 4″
  (folds to 2″ x 3½″)
1½″ Silver and ivory wire mesh craft ribbon, 3″ wide
1½" Variated color silk ribbon, ⅝″ wide
2¾″ x 1⅛″ Natural paper with botanical elements and torn edge style
2″ x ¾″ Natural white paper, with angle cut corners
½″ Abalone button
3″ Coral silk ribbon, ⅛″ wide
Thick clear-drying scrapbook paste

Apply the paste to the back of the wire mesh ribbon, then apply to placecard, centering it. Apply paste to the back of the natural paper with the botanical elements, then apply to mesh. Apply paste to the back of the natural white paper, then apply on top of botanical elements paper. Thread the ⅛" ribbon through the holes in the abalone shell button. Hot glue button overlapping the upper lefthand corner of the natural white paper by ¼"

Time: 4 minutes   **Skill Level: Beginner**   **Cost: $$**

Wire Mesh and Beaded Wire Votive Holder

Glass votive holder, 2½″ high
8″ flexible silver wire mesh, 1½″ wide
3 10″ pieces of thin gold wire

Beads:
1 3mm Gold craft bead
5 Gold mini beads
4 Purple glass beads
4 Blue glass beads
2 Green glass beads
Needlenose pliers
Votive candle

Wrap wire mesh around votive holder. Crimp in back to hold in place. One at a time, thread all three pieces of gold wire through the mesh "seam" in the back in order to hold them in place. Pull the ends around to the front. Thread beads onto wire ends. Use the pliers to crimp ends so beads don't fall off. Taking all six wire ends, twist twice in order to secure in front. Spread and fan out the wire ends.

Time: 6 minutes   **Skill Level: Beginner**   **Cost: $$**

FOURTH OF JULY

Nothing says summer quite like the Fourth of July. Visions of firework displays, picnics, and barbecues immediately run through our heads as well as fond memories of holding our first sparkler or carrying sleepy children back to the car after a long day of festivities. Being a casual holiday, this celebration calls for casual favors. Nothing elaborate or too fancy here. Tiny star-shaped blue-and-white votives are perfect to sprinkle around your table. Add a touch of red by way of foil-wrapped chocolates. You could also incorporate red into your grouping by putting tiny red roses or other flowers in the mini blue-and-white pails. We've shown them here acting as votive holders and receptacles for cheerful red candies. Miniature American flags would also add a nice patriotic touch.

A BEACH OR PATIO PARTY

The beach is such a versatile setting! It can be fun and playful, romantic, elegant, rustic, or just plain casual. Whichever motif you choose, the sand and sea will provide a perfect backdrop.

Many of us only get to the beach once in a while, or live too far away to be able to plan a party there. Consider capturing the essence of the shore in your own backyard by including beach-themed favors and decorations for your next pool party or barbecue. Use a weathered wooden lighthouse (either purchased or made from a kit) as a charming decoration or centerpiece that sets the stage. Introduce the sand and sea shell elements with charming (not to mention easy and inexpensive) placecards and votives. Or consider filling small, glass flowerpot-shaped votive holders with tiny polished rocks or miniature sea shells for a fun, outdoor effect. You can also place a votive candle in the pots first, then pour in the shells so that they fill the space between the candle and the glass, making a great votive holder. And don't be afraid to use real shells to accent your table and help set the mood.

Wooden & Raffia Topiary

Green florist foam
White and gray sea foam moss
2½″ x 2½″ Metal patina green container
Purchased 2″ diameter wood sliver-covered ball on 6″
  wire stem
12″ Strip natural-colored raffia, ½″ wide
12″ Strip mocha-colored raffia, ½″ wide

Fill container with florist foam. Apply hot glue to top of foam, press moss into hot glue, allowing to crown up around where stem will be and to fall over edges a bit.

Push stem into florist foam about 1½″ deep.

Take both strips of raffia and tie around stem, ¼″ below the base of the ball. Do not tie in a bow, but do cinch tightly. Apply a dab of hot glue in the space between the raffia and the ball. Push the tied raffia into the glue. While glue is still hot, push up and pinch the raffia just below the cinch into the hot glue in order to cover the knot.

On the raffia tails, at 1″ intervals, twist the raffia and apply just a teeny amount of hot glue to hold the twist. There should be two twists on each tail. Trim ends.

Time: 15 minutes   **Skill Level: Beginner**   **Cost: $$**

Wire Mesh and Abalone Button Collage Placecard

1 Silver-edged fold-over tent style placecard 3½″ x 4″
  (folds to 2″ x 3½″)
1½″ Silver and ivory wire mesh craft ribbon, 3″ wide
1½″ Variated color silk ribbon, ⅝″ wide
2¾″ x 1⅛″ Natural paper with botanical elements, torn-edged
2″ x ¾″ Natural white paper, with angle-cut corners
½″ Abalone button
3″ Coral silk ribbon, ⅛″ wide
Thick clear-drying scrapbook paste

Apply the paste to the back of the wire mesh ribbon, then apply to placecard, centering it. Apply paste to the back of the natural paper with the botanical elements, then apply to mesh. Apply paste to the back of the natural white paper, then apply on top of botanical elements paper. Thread the ⅛″ ribbon through the holes in the abalone shell button. Hot glue button overlapping the upper lefthand corner of the natural white paper by ¼″

Time: 4 minutes   **Skill Level: Beginner**   **Cost: $$**

Sand and Shell Placecard Holder

Matte gold Pictureframe Placecard
Clean sand
Mini shells from beach or craft store
Thick clear-drying scrapbook paste
Hot glue

Taking your finger, smear the paste in a random swirling pattern to the bottom half of the Pictureframe Placecard, going up farther on one side than the other. Sprinkle the clean sand into the paste. When dry, apply the small seashells with hot glue.

Time: 3 minutes   **Skill Level: Beginner**   **Cost: $**

Sand and Shell Votive Holder

Glass votive holder, 2½″ tall
Clean sand
Mini shells from beach or craft store
Thick clear-drying scrapbook paste
Hot glue
Votive candle

Taking your finger, smear the paste along the very bottom of the glass votive holder. Sprinkle the clean sand into the paste. When dry, apply the small seashells with hot glue.

Time: 3 minutes
Skill Level: Beginner
Cost: $$

ETCETERA

These are favors that work for a number of different categories and aren't limited to any particular occasion. There are many unusual photo holder "stands" available today and they make a wonderful, whimsical way to display your placecards. They work for office showers, fundraisers, corporate events, sales meetings, as well as dinner parties. They are something that most guests will appreciate.

Candles are one of the most versatile items ever to grace home decorating. Pillars, tapers, and votives can all be used to embellish a table, add to the general ambiance, and make a splendid favor. Tie a simple ribbon or wrap a particularly beautiful section of lace around the candle and it is transformed into a beautiful gift. Use your imagination in decorating these three-inch pillars and they will make a wonderful statement that everyone will enjoy taking home.

AN ASIAN DINNER PARTY

The Asian influence has arrived in this country in a big way. From fashion and home decorating, to philosophy and relaxation techniques, Asian influences are shaping the way we live.

There is a visual serenity to Asian aesthetics that is perfect for creating a wonderful relaxed atmosphere. The key is using elements of nature and focusing on less rather than more. Humble polished rocks become an interesting focal point, as do small seed balls displayed in a crystal bowl, with a definite minimalist, architectural feel. A topiary of miniature ornamental maple leaves makes a perfect accent for this setting. Bits of natural fiber and rice paper transform simple glass votives into beautiful Asian accents for your table and guests. Placecards using those same interesting paper elements become works of art with a definite Asian influence.

For the true craft enthusiast, or those merely wishing to explore their own creativity, the decoupage box will make a truly striking favor that your guests will cherish. Asian cultures have long been known to place as much emphasis on the container that a gift is presented in as much as the gift itself. We've taken this a step further and made a gift of the box.

Maple Leaf Topiary

3″ x 3″ Terra cotta pot

2 Sheets 8″ x 11″ natural paper

Decoupage glue

Sponge applicator

Ivory wax stick

Seal

Green florists foam

Burgundy-colored stamp pad

6″ Multi-hued brown silk ribbon, ⅝″

1 Pack brown mulberry seeds

2 3″ Diameter grapevine wreaths

6 Thin grapevine sticks (could use fewer number of sticks if they are thicker)

6 4″ Pieces of wire

1½ Yards of multi-colored miniature maple leaf garland

Hot glue

Tear natural paper into 2" x 2" strips. Apply decoupage glue to the back of each individual piece of paper. Apply to the terra cotta pot in a random pattern, covering completely. Make sure to go up and over the lip so there is no raw edge showing on the flower pot. After the pot is completely covered, apply a layer of decoupage glue over the entire thing with a sponge tip applicator in order to seal it. Let dry.

Fill pot with the florist foam. Cover foam with a layer of hot glue and sprinkle the mulberry seeds to cover.

Take the 6 grapevine twigs and twist together to form the trunk. Secure with wire at both the top and the bottom.

Take the two grapevine wreaths and place one inside the other and turn it so that it runs perpendicular to the other wreath, like a globe. Take another piece of wire and secure it at the top and bottom. Using the remaining pieces of wire, secure the double wreath to the twig trunk.

Push the trunk into the foam, going about 1½" deep. The whole topiary should stand 10½" high.

Beginning at the base, take the maple leaf garland and stab it into the foam to anchor. Twist around the trunk twice, then continue to twist your way up the stem until you reach the wreath. At the wreath, take the garland and follow the spheres, one at a time, winding it in and out so that it stays in place. You'll want to cover the wreaths evenly, and hide any wires that may show.

Loop the silk ribbon and hot glue into place. Dip seal into the rubber stamp and then press it into the melted ivory wax.

Time: 30 minutes   **Skill Level: Advanced**   **Cost: $$**

Decoupage Asian Box

Paper maché oval box, 2½″ x 2¼″
Black and gold "plaid" paper, 4″ x 4″
Natural "bark chip" paper, 2½″ x 2¼″
Natural "bark chip" paper, 2½″ x 1½″
Gold paper with stripe texture, 2½″ x 1½″
White paper with leaves, 2½″ x 1½″
White paper with gold "sponged on" pattern, 2½″ x 1½″
Ivory wax stick
Wax seal
Gold metallic stamp pad
Decoupage glue
Sponge tip applicator
Gold cylinder button, 1⅜″ long
Brown ombre silk ribbon, ½″ wide
Hot glue

Apply decoupage glue to papers, then apply to the box. Apply the gold and black plaid to lid. (Fold edges like wrapping a box and bring to inside of lid to hide.)

Apply the four 2½" x 1½" papers to the four corners of the box, with ends meeting halfway along each side. Apply the 2½" x 2¼" natural bark chip paper to the bottom of the box. Thread the ribbon through the button and hot glue onto center of lid. Make four wax seals by dipping the seal onto the gold stamp pad before pressing into the melted wax. (This gives it the metallic effect). Hot glue seals into place on the box, making sure not to place them too high so that the box lid will seat properly.

Time: 20 minutes   Skill Level: Intermediate   Cost: $$

Natural Rice Paper Votive

Glass votive holder, 2½″ high
7¼″ x 2½″ piece of rice paper
Decoupage glue
Sponge applicator
12″ Piece natural color raffia
12″ Mocha-colored raffia
Votive candle

Apply decoupage glue to the entire strip of rice paper. Wrap around votive holder. Apply a thin topcoat of the decoupage glue to seal. Twist both lengths of raffia together, then tie around votive ending with a double knot in the front. Fan ends.

Time: 5 minutes   **Skill Level: Beginner**   **Cost: $$**

Three Squares and a Feather Placecard

Ivory medium weight notecard, 3¼″ x 5¼″ with pre-cut scalloped edges

Taupe medium weight card stock, 2¾″ x 2½″

Brown natural fiber or rice paper, ⅛″ x ⅛″

Charcoal natural fiber or rice paper, ⅛″ x ⅛″

Black natural fiber or rice paper, ⅛″ x ⅛″

Brown and black craft feather, 2¾″ long, with feathers "stripped" from bottom 2″

Thick clear-drying scrapbook paste or decoupage glue

Sponge tip applicator

Fold ivory notecard into a "tent."

Trim ¼″ from top right 1⅝″ of taupe colored card stock. (See photo for exact shape.)

Apply glue or paste to back of taupe cutout and place on front of ivory notecard. Spacing evenly from the top left and angling down to the right hand corner, apply adhesive to the backs of the squares and affix on top of the taupe piece as shown.

Apply glue or paste to feather and lay across the three squares with the feather tip in the brown square with the tip extending slightly beyond the square into the taupe area.

Time: 5 minutes   **Skill Level: Beginner**   **Cost: $**

Asian Votive Holder

Glass votive holder, 2½" high
6" x 2" piece of black natural fiber paper with
    gold threads in it
Gold "crushed" paper, 1⅛" x 1⅛"
Natural colored paper with black Chinese
    characters on it, 6¾" x 1¼"
Decoupage glue
Sponge applicator
Red sealing wax
Wax seal
Votive candle
Hot glue (optional)

Apply decoupage glue to the entire strip of black paper. Wrap around votive holder. The paper will not cover completely and will leave a ⅝" strip of glass uncovered. This should go in the front. Apply glue to the square of gold paper. Apply the gold paper turned at a 45-degree angle (will look like a diamond) and center over the opening in the black paper. Apply glue to the Oriental character paper and apply around center of votive holder, placing the seam in the back. Apply sealing wax directly to votive holder and impress with seal, or make the wax seal on a piece of wax paper and hot glue into place.

Time: 7 minutes   **Skill Level: Beginner**   **Cost: $$**

Asian Character Collage Placecard

Ivory medium weight notecard, 3¼″ x 5¼″ with pre-cut scalloped
  edges
Black natural fiber paper with gold threads in it, 1⅜″ high x 3⅛″ wide
Natural colored paper with black Chinese characters on it, 1⅛″ high
  x 1½″ wide
Gold paper with stripe texture, 2⅜″ high x 1⅜″ wide
Beaded dangle
4″ Natural color silk ribbon, ⅛″ wide
Thick clear-drying scrapbook paste or decoupage glue
Sponge tip applicator
Super or Krazy Glue

Fold ivory notecard into a "tent."

Apply papers as shown, beginning with the gold, then the black, then
the Chinese character piece. Apply the glue to the back of each piece of
paper before laying them down on the notecard. Affix dangle in the upper
righthand corner of the Chinese character piece of paper with Super or
Krazy Glue. You will need to hold it in place until it "sets".

Time: 5 minutes   **Skill Level: Beginner**   **Cost: $**

GIFTS FROM THE KITCHEN

Gifts for the kitchen, especially those from your kitchen, have a special feel all their own. While flavored oils and vinegars are probably more thought of as hostess gifts, they can also make wonderful favors. The freshest of virgin olive oil or the most perfectly aged balsamic vinegar can be imbued with fresh herbs and garlic, or peppercorns. Other types of vinegar are perfectly accented with berries, peaches or other fruits. If you have a special signature salad dressing that you are known for, then make up a batch and put it in decorative bottles—your guests will be thrilled. There are plenty of fabulous bottles and containers available to make your gift beautiful to look at as well as pleasing to the taste buds. If you don't have the time to make these in your own kitchen, they're available at many gourmet shops and department stores. Whether homemade or store bought, take an extra moment—and a bit of raffia or ribbon—to decorate your container and your favor will be truly memorable.

Jams, whether made with fresh fruit in your kitchen or purchased at a store specializing in such goodies, make a sweet favor, and are especially suited to a country theme or a tea. If you have the time, a well-placed paper or silk flower and a length of interesting ribbon will make the favor stand out just that much more.

QUICK AND EASY RECIPES

Herbed Vinegar

2 Cups high-quality white wine vinegar
**½ Cup fresh herbs, firmly packed (dill, basil, rosemary, tarragon, or a
combination)**

Put herbs into a decorative bottle. Fill with vinegar and cover tightly.
Let stand in a cool dry place for at least ten days.

Fruited Vinegar

Use the above recipe, only substitute 2 cups of berries of your choice
for the herbs. After the vinegar has stood for ten days, strain it, then put
it back in the bottle.

Also consider savory or sweet butters placed into charming little
crocks. If you're known for your fabulous pesto, your guests would surely
enjoy a jar to take home with them. Homemade chutneys, salsas, desert
toppings and cheese spreads are all perfectly suited to gift giving.

Purchased Favors – Dinner Party

CHRISTMAS FAVORS

CHRISTMAS IS A SPECIAL TIME for most of us, full of warm memories, time with loved ones, and cherished traditions. Our most beloved holiday traditions evolve over time, growing and adapting to accommodate the changing needs of our families and our lives. In households with young children, Christmas is usually experienced at a frenetic pace as eager tots anticipate their way to Christmas morning. Certainly Christmas celebrations are most often designed to include small children. Their innocence and anticipation capture the very essence of the holiday and in turn adds to our own enjoyment. Making parties kid friendly and child proof will go a long way toward relieving some of the holiday stress.

For keeping holiday celebrations simple, there are lots of easy, streamlined favor ideas to choose from. Consider small decorated Christmas trees, glass dishes full of colorful, festive candies, or small decorated (and decorative) wreaths that can be easily purchased.

Another very simple touch is to wrap your holiday napkins with a ribbon that is attached to a beautiful Christmas tree ornament that your guests can take home with them.

Oftentimes we become so wrapped up in the chaotic hustle and bustle of the holiday that we find we have too little time to enjoy the things that really matter to us. For your next Christmas season, resolve to put aside at least one tradition that has ceased to have personal meaning for you and use that time to indulge yourself in a relaxed and cherished evening with friends and family.

Christmas Girl Placecard

Ivory medium weight notecard, 3¼″ x 5¼″ with deckled edge
Old fashioned "paper doll," 3¼″ x 1″
Red natural fiber paper, 2¼″ x 2¾″
Newsprint with torn edges, approximately 1″ square
Three buttons, 2 in ivory, 1 in blue, approximately ½″ diameter
Thick clear-drying scrapbook paste
Sponge tip applicator

Fold card in half along the 3¼″ edge. Turn so the fold is on the lefthand side of the card. Apply paste to back side of red paper and apply to center of front of card. Tear small piece of newsprint into two irregular shaped pieces, one about ¾″ square and the other about ¼″ square. Apply paste to the back of those pieces and place on the red paper. Glue the paper doll on the far righthand side of the card, slightly overlapping the edge where the red paper ends and going onto the ivory card. Put a thick dab of glue on the bottom lefthand corner of the card and arrange buttons in the glue.

Time: 7 Minutes   **Skill Level: Beginner**   **Cost: $**

Small Christmas Wreath

1 3″ Diameter grapevine wreath
3 2½″ Fake paper evergreen branches, ¼″ wide
3 Paper mistletoe leaves, ½″ long by ¼″ wide
2 Green beads, ⅜″ diameter
1 Red bead, ⅜″ diameter
2 Miniature red beads, ⅛″ diameter
36″ Thin gold craft wire
Toothpick
Hot glue
1″ x 1½″ deckle edged tag
Gold pen

Grasp evergreen branches in your fingers and pinch in the center. Arrange them so that the ends on both sides are staggered, then twist to hold. Hot glue the evergreen cluster to the top of the wreath.

Take 12" length of the wire and wrap tightly around a toothpick for curly-cue effect. It should measure 6" when finished. Form the piece into a bow, twisting instead of knotting in the center. Thread a red bead on one tail of the bow and a green bead on the other. Place a thick dab of hot glue in the enter of the evergreen cluster. Press the three mistletoe leaves on top of the evergreen, making sure to cover the "pinched" area. Apply another spot of glue and press the wire bow into that. Where the "knot" would be on a normal ribbon, glue the remaining large green bead in the center and the two smaller red beads on either side of that.

Take 20" length of wire and wrap around a toothpick as above until it measures 10". Beginning at the top right, just past the evergreen branches, weave the wire around the wreath, ending at the top left. Take the remaining 4" of wire, wrap around a toothpick for curly-cues, thread 1" x 1½" tag onto this wire and secure on wreath.

Time: 10 Minutes   **Skill Level: Beginner**   **Cost: $**

A WHITE CHRISTMAS

Nothing conveys a winter wonderland quite as effectively as the magical combination of white and silver. Perhaps it evokes the magical feeling of moonlight on freshly fallen snow, or maybe it's the sparkle of the colors that appeal to us. Whatever the reason, there are lots of favor ideas to emphasize this theme. Small silver frames make perfect placecards and require minimal effort. If you're feeling exceptionally festive, you can wrap the frame like a present or add a white silk poinsettia. Fill a white and silver porcelain box with silver-colored candy, or put out wire meshed votives for your guests to take home. Silver bells, silver trays of chocolate truffles, and silver baskets filled with treats all work wonderfully for the Christmas season.

If you're wanting to make something yourself, consider creating a glass votive that shimmers with the magic iridescence of Christmas, or capture the playfulness of snowflakes on your placecards. Cover a paper maché, tree-shaped box with a layer of white and silver paint or, for those who really relish a fun project, consider our White Christmas Tree Topiary to add a striking presence to your table.

Silver Christmas Tree Topiary

Small 2″ terra cotta flower pot

Silver leaf

Decoupage glue

Sponge tip applicator

Florist foam

40″ Silver cording

10 White leaves about 2″ long with silver patina

Iridescent glitter

1 Purchased white 5″ Christmas tree element (can be found in miniature Christmas village sections of craft and hobby stores)

40 Beads in a variety of sizes and colors (we used matte silver, pearl, and iridescent clear)

Hot glue

Completely cover the terra cotta pot with decoupage glue. Apply silver leaf with sponge tip applicator to press on and crinkle. When completely covered, apply a coat of decoupage glue to seal. Before glue is dry, sprinkle the pot with iridescent glitter.

Fill silver-leafed pot with florist foam, level with top edge of pot. The tree we used had a 2" base on the tree so we covered this with hot glue and pushed it into the foam.

Beginning at the base of the tree, secure cording with hot glue and wind up the tree, going around five times, ending at the top with a length of 7". As you go, push the cording "into" the tree branches to secure. At the top, unravel the final 7", then fold cording forward to form a ½" high loop, securing in place with a dab of hot glue. Put a bead at that joint to cover glue. Let the unraveled tails cascade down the tree.

Take the white leaves and, one at a time, apply hot glue to the back of the leaf. Press leaf onto the Christmas tree base, with one end up against the tree "trunk" and the other end hanging over the edge of the flower pot by about ½". Make sure and overlap the leaves as you lay them down so that the entire base of the tree is covered and will not show through.

Take a pinch of decoupage glue on the corner of the sponge applicator and "sponge" the glue on the tips of the leaves. Then apply iridescent glitter so that it adheres in the glue spots.

Time: 30 minutes   **Skill Level: Intermediate**   **Cost:$$$**

Snowflake Placecard I

White Pictureframe Placecard
Thick clear-drying scrapbook paste
White and silver snowflake confetti

Apply glue to top righthand corner of placecard. Pile on confetti, (approximately 8–10 individual snowflakes) adding more paste as necessary to achieve a stacked effect. Repeat this process using four or five snowflakes in the bottom lefthand corner.

Time: 2 Minutes
Skill Level: Beginner
Cost: $

Snowflake Placecard II

1 Silver-edged fold-over tent style place card 3½″ x 4″
   (folds to 2″ x 3½″)
Snowflake confetti
Thick clear-drying scrapbook paste

Fold placecard into tent. Place glue on back of snowflakes and place two in the bottom left corner. Glue eleven in the top right corner forming a wave. Place snowflakes on top of each other to give a dimensional effect.

Time: 2 Minutes
Skill Level: Beginner
Cost: $

Iridescent Snow Votive

Glass flowerpot style votive, either clear or
   frosted
Medium-size iridescent glitter
Decoupage glue
White votive candle
Masking tape
Spray matte sealer

Apply glue to the bottom of the flowerpot
from the lip down. Keep the lip clear of glue and
glitter for a contrast effect. Sprinkle the glitter
into the wet glue. Let dry. Cover the clear lip with
masking tape, and spray with a matte sealer to
seal in the glitter.

Time: 6 Minutes   **Skill Level: Beginner**   **Cost: $$**

Silver Leaf Votive
Candle Cube

Square votive candle, 2″
Matte drying decoupage glue
Silver Leafing — 15–16 nickel size pieces
Sponge tip applicator
Tweezers

Apply decoupage glue to the four sides of the candle as well as the top.
Using the tweezers, if necessary, apply the leafing to the candle, then use
the sponge tip applicator to pat down and crinkle. When finished, apply
a thin coat of decoupage glue over the entire candle to seal.

Time: 3 minutes   **Skill Level: Beginner**   **Cost: $**

Silver Truffle Tray

Silver coaster
13″ Diameter circle of tulle
20″ Length of ⅝″ satin-edged organza ribbon
20″ Length of silver cord
19″ Length of silver cord
1″ Diameter silk flower
2″ White cloth-covered wire
Three chocolate truffles

Cut 13″ circle from tulle.

Lay flat, then place the coaster on top of the tulle circle, making sure it is centered.

Place the three truffles on the coaster.

Gather up the tulle over the truffles and twist to gather. Hold the gather in place with the 2″ wire.

Holding both lengths of silver cord, wrap twice around the gather then tie once to hold (Do not tie into a bow yet!).

Tie ribbon around the gather directly on top of silver cording. When knotting the ribbon, make sure to loop one "tail" of the silver cording through the ribbon in order to merge the two together.

Holding all three pieces (both cord lengths and the length of ribbon), tie into a bow. Adjust the lengths.

Knot the end of the cording and trim the edge of the ribbon.

Hot glue flower onto the knot of the bow.

Time: 4 minutes   Skill Level: Beginner   Cost: $$$

Silver Basket

Silver basket
13″ Circle of white tulle
20″ Length of ⅝″ satin edged organza ribbon
8″ String of miniature pearls
15 Silver wrapped chocolates
Hot glue

Place the candy in the center of the tulle. Gather up the tulle and secure with the ribbon. Tie ribbon into a bow. Trim ends. Form three loops with the pearl strand and hot glue into place on the top of the bow knot. Place in basket.

Time: 4 minutes
Skill Level: Beginner
Cost: $$$

Silver Christmas Bell

Silverplated bell
16″ Sheer white organza ribbon with silver edge, ⅞″ wide
2 Pieces soft silver mesh fabric or ribbon, 3″ x 2″

Bring the white organza ribbon around bell handle to the front to tie. Form one of the loops for the bow and, before completing the bow, lay the two pieces of silver mesh on top of the first loop, then finish the bow. This will result in a bow with two additional silver mesh 'tails' on either side of the it.

Time: 2 minutes   **Skill Level: Beginner**   **Cost: $$$**

Christmas Tree Box

Paper maché box in shape of Christmas tree
Gold acrylic paint
Silver acrylic paint
Gold ink pen
Sponge brush
Iridescent glitter
Decoupage glue

Paint the entire box and lid, inside and out, with the silver paint. Let dry. Dip the sponge tip applicator in gold paint, and VERY SOFTLY and sparingly accent the top of the lid with faint swipes of gold. Let dry. Using the sponge tip applicator, dab a bit of decoupage glue on the points of the tree. Sprinkle the glitter. Let dry.

Time: 15 minutes   **Skill Level: Beginner**   **Cost: $**

CHRISTMAS DINNER

Votives are an adaptable, easy-to-make favor and provide a wide variety of ways for you to create fun, festive holiday favors for your guests. String beads on wire and wrap them around the glass in a variety of ways or consider sprinkling holiday colored beads onto the bottom edge of a votive. A festive holiday bow affixed to a goblet style votive holder or a candleholder wrapped in a Christmas-themed vellum paper are two more easy ways to give your guests a favor with a holiday touch.

Christmas "collage" placecards are a fun project that the whole family can become involved in. Bits of holiday ribbon, Christmas stickers, buttons, pieces of Christmas cards or wrapping paper, even canceled holiday stamps all lend themselves to this fun, creative, easy art form.

And who wouldn't appreciate a beautiful holiday sachet filled with a heavenly, Christmas scented potpourri mix?

Goblet Votive with Christmas Bow

Glass goblet style votive, 4″ high
2 Five-inch pieces of floral wire
20″ Wired, French ribbon in
 Christmas plaid, 2″ wide
3 White and gold leaves, 1½″ – 2″ long
4 Three-inch-long paper evergreen
 sprigs
2 Red and gold wire ball clusters
Hot glue
Votive candle

Make bow by taking the 20″ piece of ribbon and forming a loop around your thumb. Then bring your index finger in to pinch the loop. Twist the ribbon at the center and form a 1½″ loop to the right of the center, twist and pinch at center back with index finger, then form a 1½″ loop to the left of the center. Twist at the back and pinch with the other twists. Repeat the last two steps forming a 2½″ loop this time, ending with the 'tail' about ½″ past the center in the back. Slide wire through the middle of the top loop, and secure all the layers together by twisting. Take two of the evergreen sprigs, one of the wire ball clusters, and one of the leaves. Twist together to form a cluster. Repeat with the remaining elements, this time using two leaves. Twist to secure. Turn both clusters with wire ends to the center, secure to the bow with the last piece of wire. Hot glue the entire cluster to the votive, making sure to tilt it at an angle.

Time: 10 minutes   Skill Level: Intermediate   Cost: $$

Bead Trimmed Votive

Glass votive cup with flared lip, 2″ high
Bead mixture including red, green, gold, and white beads
¾″ Wide double-sided super sticky craft tape
Votive candle

Make sure votive cup is clean before starting. Apply tape around bottom edge of votive. Sprinkle beads onto tape and press into place to make sure they adhere securely.

Time: 2 minutes   **Skill Level: Beginner**   **Cost: $$**

Vellum Wrapped Votive

Glass votive cup, 2″ in diameter and 2½″ high
Vellum, 2½″ wide x 7¼″ long, cut straight or with deckled edge
Votive candle
Super sticky double-sided craft tape

Wrap vellum around glass votive, affixing in back with special craft quality "super sticky" double-faced tape.

Time: 2 minutes   **Skill Level: Beginner**   **Cost: $$**

Bead Draped Goblet Votive

Glass goblet style votive, 4″ high
3 24″ Lengths of gold craft wire
¼ Cup of glass beads in Christmas colors, with varied sizes
Toothpick
Hot glue gun
Votive candle

Slide the beads onto one of the 24″ lengths of wire leaving 2″ at end. Twist that 2″ end around a toothpick to form a curly, spring effect. Twist second and third wires around the first beaded wire, twisting and "springing" with a toothpick at approximately 1½″ intervals. Leave a spring tail to secure around the base of the holder. Take the entire three strands in your hand and wrap them around the votive in a spiral effect. Begin at the top and allow to fold over the lip and hot glue in place inside the votive cup. When you spiral down to the base of the votive holder, secure the wire at the trunk of the votive with dabs of hot glue.

Time: 25 minutes   **Skill Level: Intermediate**   **Cost: $$**

Beaded Wire Wrapped Flowerpot Votive

Glass flowerpot votive, 2½″ high
2 14″ Lengths of gold craft wire
⅓ Cup craft beads in Christmas colors, with varied sizes
Toothpick
Hot glue
Votive candle

String beads onto both wires, keeping the last ¾″ of each end free of beads. Fold over ends to temporarily keep beads from falling off.

Find center of each wire and move beads out of the way. Twist wires together at identified center points. Hot glue this twist to the back of the votive, just under the 'lip'. Wrap the beaded wires around to the front of the votive, twisting twice along the way. When you reach the front, form two 1″ loops of the beaded wire and position them so they are hanging down. Twist wire to secure. Wrap the ¾″ wire ends around a toothpick to form curly-cues. Crimp edges. Secure in front with a dab of hot glue.

Time: 20 minutes   **Skill Level: Beginner**   **Cost: $$**

Christmas Collage Placecard

Ivory medium weight notecard, 3¼″ x 5¼″ with deckled edge
5¾″ Gold metallic mesh ribbon, 1½″ wide
8½″ Green mesh ribbon, ⅝″ wide
Christmas sticker, approximately 1½″ x 2″
10 mini craft beads in Christmas colors
Thick clear-drying scrapbook paste
Sponge tip applicator

Fold card in half like a tent. Cut green ribbon into two pieces, one 3¼″ long and the other 5″ long.

Apply scrapbook paste to the gold ribbon and place it ⅝″ from left side of card along the long edge. Fold raw edges of ribbon to inside of card and secure with glue.

Apply paste to the back of the 5″ piece of green ribbon and apply down the center of the gold mesh ribbon. Cut the tails of the ribbon in an inverted V.

Apply paste to the back of the 3¼″ piece of green ribbon and lay across the face of the card, about ¾″ down from the top fold.

Using the paste, apply the sticker on top of the ribbons, across the face of the card, about ¾″ from the left edge of the card and ¼″ down from the fold at the top.

Place a dab of the paste at the top left and bottom right corners of the sticker. Press beads into the glue. Let dry.

Time: 10 minutes   Skill Level: Beginner   Cost: $

Pretty Corner Sachet Pocket

10″ Square fabric
10″ Square inexpensive sheer fabric
¾ Cup dried flower potpourri
Hot glue
16″ Sheer organza ribbon in dark rose, ⅝″ wide
Organza flower

Cut 10″ square of fabric Place on table with wrong side up.

Fold all edges over ¼″, press, then use hot glue to glue them in place.

Cut 10″ piece of inexpensive, sheer fabric.

Lay flat on table, wrong side up, and fill with ¾ cup of pretty dried flower potpourri.

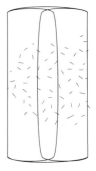

Fold both sides to middle, overlapping about 1 – 2".

Repeat with top and bottom to form a wrapped packet of about 3 – 3½". Hot glue packet closed.

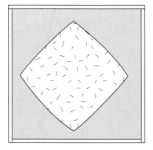

Place sheer packet fold-side down in the center of the finished-edge fabric from step one. Finished-edge fabric should be wrong-side up, and packet should sit on the wrong side.

Place a dab of hot glue smaller than a dime onto the center of the sheerpacket. Bring four corners of outside fabric into the middle.

Press each of the four corners into the hot glue. Fabric should sink down into center glue spot.

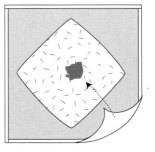

Using the hot glue, affix the deep rose ribbon, then glue the organza flowers on top of that.

Time: 10–12 minutes   Skill Level: Intermediate   Cost: $–$$

AN ELEGANT CHRISTMAS
STOCKING FAVOR

Occasionally we find ourselves with a little extra time at the holidays coinciding with a desire to create something really special with our hands, something to give to our loved ones. If that's the case, you might consider this pressed and gilded velvet stocking filled with old-fashioned candy sticks as the perfect accent to your Christmas table.

If you don't have quite that much time, your guests will never know and they will enjoy the festive collage placecard shown here as an alternative.

Cut Velvet Christmas Stocking

2 Pieces of wine colored velvet, 4½″ x 7″
3¼″ x 6½″ white brocade satin
13″ Sheer white organza ribbon, ¼″ wide
14″ Sheer green organza ribbon, ½″ wide
13″ Gold craft wire
Beads to decorate wire
Poinsettia rubber stamp
Metallic gold acrylic paint
Small paint brush
Iron

To emboss stocking:

On one piece of the velvet, spritz with water. Take brush and dab random bits of the gold paint onto the rubber stamp pad. Place the rubber pad upside down with the painted rubber side facing you. Place the RIGHT side of the velvet on the painted stamp. Take a hot iron (no steam) and press down hard so that the velvet will crush. Hold for a count of four. Release.

To make stocking:

Trace pattern from page 188 and cut both pieces of velvet to fit the pattern. Position the stocking pattern so that it best displays your embossing.

Lay cut stocking pieces RIGHT sides together. Stitch, using a ¼″ seam allowance. Snip in toward seam at all curves to allow a smoother look.

Turn right side out and finger press to smooth seams. Turn right side in again.

Fold cuff lengthwise, RIGHT sides together.

Stitch the two short ends. Turn right side out.

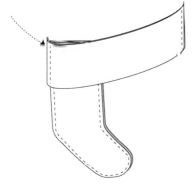

With the RIGHT side of the cuff laying against the WRONG side of the stocking, inside lay the cuff on top of the inside-out stocking so that the raw edges are level with the top edge of the stocking. The ends will overlap about ¼".

Stitch the cuff to the stocking, using a ¼" seam allowance.

Fold the cuff over to lay down on the top of the stocking. Turn the stocking inside out.

Cut the wire into a 4" piece and a 9" piece.

Take both pieces of ribbon and lay them in your hand. 3" from one end, pinch your finger and make a 1" loop above the pinch. Make another loop, then a third. This should leave you with another 3" tail. Pinching at loops, take the 9" piece of wire and center it, then wrap it around the pinch three times to secure. There should be two straight, 4" pieces of wire left on each side of loop cluster.

Twist these 4" ends of wire around a toothpick to "curl". Thread beads and pearl onto wire. Crimp end with needlenose pliers to secure.

Center the 4" piece of wire behind loop and repeat the procedure with it.

Time: 30 minutes   **Skill Level: Intermediate**   **Cost: $–$$**

Stocking
Tracing Pattern

Green Fiber Paper Collage Placecard

1 Placecard, fold-over tent style measuring $3\frac{1}{2}''$ x $4''$ (folds to $2''$ x $3\frac{1}{2}''$)
$3\frac{1}{2}''$ x $4''$ Piece of green natural fiber paper
$2\frac{1}{2}''$ x $1\frac{1}{2}''$ Gold metallic paper with stripe texture
1 Christmas sticker measuring $1\frac{5}{8}''$ x $1''$
1 Miniature holly cluster with 2 leaves and 2 berries
$4\frac{1}{2}''$ Woven Christmas ribbon in green, red and gold, $\frac{1}{8}''$ wide
Thick clear-drying scrapbook paste
Sponge tip applicator
Hot glue

Put the paste on the back side of the green fiber paper and place it over the entire front of the placecard. Make sure you position the placecard so the fold goes in the correct direction. Apply paste to the gold piece of paper and position on the front of the green covered placecard $\frac{1}{16}''$ from the left edge of the card and $\frac{1}{16}''$ from the top fold of the card. Apply sticker $\frac{1}{16}''$ from the fold in the upper right corner of the card, and $\frac{1}{16}''$ from right edge. Use hot glue to apply holly cluster in place at the top left corner of the gold paper.

Time: 5 minutes   Skill Level: Beginner   Cost: $

A GOLDEN CHRISTMAS

The depth and richness of gold are a perfect accent for the Christmas holidays, adding touches of gilding to the festivities. You can capture this color and bring it to your table in myriad ways, from gold rimmed plates, to a subtle golden thread running through your holiday napkins. Almonds coated in gold or sheer gold organza ribbon are more easy ways to bring the merest hint of opulence to your setting. Since Christmas can be such a hectic time for most people, we've included many favors on these pages that need only be picked up at the store in order to be ready for giving. The pearl snowflake ornament on the napkin would make a nice addition to your guests' trees. Rustic cinnamon sticks need only be tied with an elegant ribbon for a quick, easy and delightful smelling favor. Or who could resist a beautiful golden box, just begging to be opened?

Votives are especially appropriate during the holidays. Many people who don't light a single candle all year bring them out at Christmas time. Consider purchased golden pots filled with wax, or golden wire mesh votive holders. If you have the time to decorate them yourself, consider our simple wire accented votive, a gold and silver leaf votive bowl, or a festive star and swirl decoupaged candle pot.

Gold Star Decoupaged Votive Holder

Frosted glass flowerpot votive, 3″ high

White natural fiber paper with copper stars, 9″ x 2¼″

Golden pen paint marker (able to write on glass)

Silver pen paint marker (able to write on glass)

Decoupage glue

Sponge applicator

Votive candle

Apply decoupage glue to the bottom section of the glass flowerpot. Wrap the strip of the tissue paper around the glue-covered bottom section. Apply a thin layer of decoupage glue over the top of the tissue paper to seal. Let dry. Using the gold paint pen, draw eleven gold swirls, evenly spaced and alternating position from top to bottom, along the lip of the pot. Then take the silver pen and make six little three-dot groupings between the swirls.

Time: 10 minutes   **Skill Level: Beginner**   **Cost: $$**

Gold Wire Wrapped Flowerpot Votive

(pictured on the opposite page)

Glass flowerpot votive, 3″ high

7 15″ Cuts of gold craft wire

Hot glue

Votive candle

Lay all the wire pieces together and twist at center. Secure this twist to the center back of the flowerpot lip with hot glue. Bring all the wires to the front, twist, then knot once. Let tails hand down, fanning them out and slightly bending the ends.

Time: 2 minutes   **Skill Level: Beginner**   **Cost: $$**

Gold and Silver Leafed Votive Bowl

Bowl-shaped glass votive holder, 2″
Matte drying decoupage glue
Gold and silver leafing
Sponge tip applicator
Tweezers
Votive candle

Apply decoupage glue to the votive holder. Using the tweezers, if necessary, apply the leafing to the glass, then use the sponge tip applicator to pat down and crinkle. When finished, apply a thin coat of decoupage glue over the entire votive to seal.

Time: 7 minutes   Skill Level: Beginner   Cost: $$

Carla

Mr. & Mrs.
Richard Grimes
Table 5

Beverly

Jennifer

NEW YEAR'S EVE

The most common celebration for ringing out the old and bringing in the new is probably the cocktail party or late night buffet. There will be times, however, when an all-out dinner party is exactly what you're in the mood for. If that's the case, consider the festive, jewel-toned favors we've shown here. Once again we've used the very easy but striking technique of offering an ornament on pretty napkins. A frosted, bejeweled votive casts a merry glow around your table, and these magnificent, bejeweled placecards are practically works of art!

Whatever favor you choose, it might be a fun idea to commemorate the date with a liquid paint pen somewhere on the bottom or back of these favors. It's a nice way to mark the passage of old Father Time.

Bejeweled Placecards

Pictureframe Placecards
Plastic jewels in a variety of shapes, sizes, and colors
Super or Krazy Glue
Metal charms for top ornament
**(NOTE: Metal charms can be used, small pieces from old jewelry, stiff
 golden fabric appliques — let your imagination run free here.)**

NOTE: For these placecards you will absolutely need to write the
names on the cards and insert them into the frame before decorating. For
an added elegant touch, consider finishing the calligraphied cards with a
gold crackle finish or the lightest touch of gold glitter.

Place Super or Krazy Glue on the main top ornament and place at the
top center of the frame. Place a drop of glue on each jewel and place on
frame. You can either completely cover the surface, or place jewels to
outline the oval opening. Let your imagination go wild!

Time: 10 minutes   **Skill Level: Beginner**   **Cost: $–$$**

Crystal Mosaic Votive Holder

Frosted glass votive cup, 2½″ in diameter and 3″ high
13 Multi-colored square decorative crystals approximately. ⅜″
   (available in craft or fabric store)
Glass adhesive in tube
Votive candle

Apply glue to the lip of the flowerpot. NOTE: The glue will turn the frosted glass clear. This is okay since this gives it a nice textural variation. Place the crystals evenly spaced around the lip, alternating top and bottom placement with each crystal. You will need to hold each crystal in place for a few seconds so that it doesn't slip off.

Time: 6 minutes   **Skill Level: Beginner**   **Cost: $$**

Purchased Favors — Christmas

Christmas — Page 164
    Star Shaped Ornaments $
    Old Fashioned Candy Stick $$
    Small Christmas Trees $$

A White Christmas — Page 168
    Silver Wire Mesh Votive $$
    Silver Frames $$–$$$$
    Porcelain Box $$$
    Glass Christmas Tree $$

A Golden Christmas — Page 190
    Gold Pot filled with Wax $$
    Golden Box $$$$
    Snowflake Ornament $$$
    Candy Covered Spoon $
    Gold Wire Mesh Votive $$

New Year's Eve — Page 194
    New Year's Ornaments $$$
    Square Frosted Votives $$
    Silver Frame $$$

THIRTY-MINUTE SPECIALS

NEVER LET LACK OF TIME be a reason for not including favors in your celebration!

The favors listed here can be made very quickly — one dozen in only thirty minutes. It's essential to have all the materials laid out beforehand, then put the favors together in an assembly line fashion. For example, cut all the lengths of ribbon or beaded trimming first, then move on to the next step in the instructions.

Thirty-Minute Specials

FAVORS ON A BUDGET

FAVORS DON'T HAVE TO BE EXPENSIVE in order to be memorable and meaningful to your guests! Placecards in particular can be quite striking with a minimal investment. Here we've listed favors that can be put together for $2.00 or less each. Another effective cost saver is to watch for sales and try to pick up votive holders or candles at 40% – 50% off. If you can do that, then the majority of the votive holders in this book will come in very close to that $2.00 limit.

Favors on a Budget

INDEX

Entertaining Log

Date _____ Time _____
Occasion/Theme *Pastors 30th Anniversary Dinner*
Number of Guests _____ Rentals _____
Decorations *Ivy Bowls c̄ floating candles*
Favors _____
Ribbon: Pastor & Mrs James Harris 30th Anniversary

Menu

Appetizers _____
Main Course _____
_____
_____
_____
Dessert _____
Wines _____

Guest List

_____ _____
_____ _____
_____ _____
_____ _____
_____ _____
_____ _____
_____ _____
_____ _____
_____ _____
_____ _____

Notes _____
_____
_____
_____

Entertaining Log

Date _____ Time _____

Occasion/Theme _____

Number of Guests _____ Rentals _____

Decorations _____

Favors _____

Menu

Appetizers _____

Main Course _____

_____

_____

_____

Dessert _____

Wines _____

Guest List

_____ _____

_____ _____

_____ _____

_____ _____

_____ _____

_____ _____

_____ _____

_____ _____

_____ _____

_____ _____

Notes _____

_____

_____

_____

Entertaining Log

Date _____ Time _____

Occasion/Theme _____

Number of Guests _____ Rentals _____

Decorations _____

Favors _____

Menu

Appetizers _____

Main Course _____

_____

_____

_____

Dessert _____

Wines _____

Guest List

_____ _____
_____ _____
_____ _____
_____ _____
_____ _____
_____ _____
_____ _____
_____ _____
_____ _____
_____ _____

Notes _____

_____

_____

_____

Entertaining Log

Date _____ Time _____

Occasion/Theme _____

Number of Guests _____ Rentals _____

Decorations _____

Favors _____

Menu

Appetizers _____

Main Course _____

_____

_____

_____

Dessert _____

Wines _____

Guest List

_____   _____

_____   _____

_____   _____

_____   _____

_____   _____

_____   _____

_____   _____

_____   _____

_____   _____

Notes _____

_____

_____

_____

Entertaining Log

Date _____ Time _____

Occasion/Theme _____

Number of Guests _____ Rentals _____

Decorations _____

Favors _____

Menu

Appetizers _____

Main Course _____

_____

_____

_____

Dessert _____

Wines _____

Guest List

_____ _____

_____ _____

_____ _____

_____ _____

_____ _____

_____ _____

_____ _____

_____ _____

_____ _____

_____ _____

Notes _____

_____

_____

_____

Entertaining Log

Date _____ Time _____

Occasion/Theme _____

Number of Guests _____ Rentals _____

Decorations _____

Favors _____

Menu

Appetizers _____

Main Course _____

_____

_____

_____

Dessert _____

Wines _____

Guest List

_____   _____

_____   _____

_____   _____

_____   _____

_____   _____

_____   _____

_____   _____

_____   _____

_____   _____

Notes _____

_____

_____

_____

Entertaining Log

Date _____ Time _____

Occasion/Theme _____

Number of Guests _____ Rentals _____

Decorations _____

Favors _____

Menu

Appetizers _____

Main Course _____

_____

_____

_____

Dessert _____

Wines _____

Guest List

_____   _____

_____   _____

_____   _____

_____   _____

_____   _____

_____   _____

_____   _____

_____   _____

_____   _____

_____   _____

Notes _____

_____

_____

_____

Entertaining Log

Date _____ Time _____

Occasion/Theme _____

Number of Guests _____ Rentals _____

Decorations _____

Favors _____

Menu

Appetizers _____

Main Course _____

_____

_____

_____

Dessert _____

Wines _____

Guest List

_____   _____

_____   _____

_____   _____

_____   _____

_____   _____

_____   _____

_____   _____

_____   _____

_____   _____

Notes _____

_____

_____

_____

Entertaining Log

Date _____   Time _____

Occasion/Theme _____

Number of Guests _____   Rentals _____

Decorations _____

Favors _____

Menu

Appetizers _____

Main Course _____

_____

_____

_____

Dessert _____

Wines _____

Guest List

_____   _____

_____   _____

_____   _____

_____   _____

_____   _____

_____   _____

_____   _____

_____   _____

_____   _____

_____   _____

Notes _____

_____

_____

_____

Entertaining Log

Date _____ Time _____

Occasion/Theme _____

Number of Guests _____ Rentals _____

Decorations _____

Favors _____

Menu

Appetizers _____

Main Course _____

_____

_____

_____

Dessert _____

Wines _____

Guest List

_____ _____

_____ _____

_____ _____

_____ _____

_____ _____

_____ _____

_____ _____

_____ _____

_____ _____

Notes _____

_____

_____

_____

Entertaining Log

Date _____ Time _____

Occasion/Theme _____

Number of Guests _____ Rentals _____

Decorations _____

Favors _____

Menu

Appetizers _____

Main Course _____

_____

_____

_____

Dessert _____

Wines _____

Guest List

_____ _____

_____ _____

_____ _____

_____ _____

_____ _____

_____ _____

_____ _____

_____ _____

_____ _____

Notes _____

_____

_____

_____

Entertaining Log

Date _____ Time _____

Occasion/Theme _____

Number of Guests _____ Rentals _____

Decorations _____

Favors _____

Menu

Appetizers _____

Main Course _____

_____

_____

_____

Dessert _____

Wines _____

Guest List

_____ _____

_____ _____

_____ _____

_____ _____

_____ _____

_____ _____

_____ _____

_____ _____

_____ _____

Notes _____

_____

_____

_____

Entertaining Log

Date _____ Time _____

Occasion/Theme _____

Number of Guests _____ Rentals _____

Decorations _____

Favors _____

Menu

Appetizers _____

Main Course _____

_____

_____

Dessert _____

Wines _____

Guest List

_____   _____

_____   _____

_____   _____

_____   _____

_____   _____

_____   _____

_____   _____

_____   _____

_____   _____

_____   _____

Notes _____

_____

_____

_____

Entertaining Log

Date _____ Time _____

Occasion/Theme _____

Number of Guests _____ Rentals _____

Decorations _____

Favors _____

Menu

Appetizers _____

Main Course _____

_____

_____

_____

Dessert _____

Wines _____

Guest List

_____   _____

_____   _____

_____   _____

_____   _____

_____   _____

_____   _____

_____   _____

_____   _____

_____   _____

Notes _____

_____

_____

_____